EARLY CHILDHO

Sharon Ryan, *Editor*

ADVISORY BOARD: *Celia Genishi, Doris Fromberg, Carrie Lobman, Rachel Theilheimer, Dominic Gullo, Amita Gupta, Beatrice Fennimore, Sue Grieshaber, Jackie Marsh, Mindy Blaise, Gail Yuen, Alice Honig, Betty Jones, Stephanie Feeney, Stacie G. Goffin, Beth Graue*

To look for other titles in this series, visit www.tcpress.com

(continued)

EXPLORING MATHEMATICS
Through
PLAY
in the Early
CHILDHOOD
CLASSROOM

AMY NOELLE PARKS

Foreword by Elizabeth Graue

TEACHERS COLLEGE PRESS

TEACHERS COLLEGE | COLUMBIA UNIVERSITY
NEW YORK AND LONDON

NATIONAL COUNCIL OF
TEACHERS OF MATHEMATICS

1906 Association Drive
Reston, VA 20191
www.nctm.org

Published simultaneously by Teachers College Press, 1234 Amsterdam Avenue, New York, NY 10027, and National Council of Teachers of Mathematics, 1906 Association Drive, Reston, VA 20191.

This material is based on work supported by the National Science Foundation under Grant No. 0844445. Any opinions, findings, and conclusions or recommendations expressed in this material are those of the author and do not necessarily reflect the views of the National Science Foundation.

Photos 1.1, 4.1, 4.2, 4.4, 5.1, 9.3, and 10.2 are by Diana Chang Blom
Photos 2.1, 2.2, 2.3, 4.3, 4.5, 4.6, 6.1, and 10.1 are by Amy Noelle Parks

Library of Congress Cataloging-in-Publication Data

Parks, Amy Noelle, author.
   Exploring mathematics through play in the early childhood classroom / Amy
      Noelle Parks ; foreword by Beth Graue.
         pages cm. — (Early childhood education series)
      Includes bibliographical references and index.
      ISBN 978-0-8077-5589-1 (pbk. : acid-free paper)
      ISBN 978-0-8077-7347-5 (e-book)
         1. Mathematics—Study and teaching (Early childhood)—Activity programs.
      I. Title.
      QA135.6.P378 2015
      372.7—dc23   2014028765

ISBN 978-0-8077-5589-1 (paper)
ISBN 978-0-8077-7347-5 (ebook)
NCTM Stock Number: 14995

Printed on acid-free paper
Manufactured in the United States of America

For Sophie and Chloe, who love to play

Contents

Foreword

Unless you are an early childhood educator, you really can't comprehend just how difficult the job is. Like most experts, a gifted early childhood teacher makes the work look so easy—pull out some toys and play—that's it, right? In *Exploring Mathematics Through Play in the Early Childhood Classroom*, Amy Parks has given us a window on how intellectually complex a play-based program can be. And it comes at exactly the right time, when, in a cruel twist of fate, we are seeing that years of selling the importance of early childhood programs has resulted in incredible investment in high-quality programs and the very practices that made early childhood unique going by the wayside. In our accountability culture, the public seems to have set up a wall between the notions of play and learning, with most elementary schools ending up as play deserts. The trend is seeping into preschool as parents and policymakers look for academic activities that make their investments likely to pay off.

Through painstaking fieldwork across multiple years, Parks has documented how children infuse mathematics into their play while playing their way into mathematics. Her rich descriptions of their interactions and photographs of children in play help us see the powerful thinking with common classroom materials. These descriptions shine a light on the potential learning embedded in children's play that might be missed by an adult unfamiliar with high-quality early childhood practices and a solid understanding of early mathematics.

Equally important, Parks pairs these portraits with descriptions of the kinds of work that teachers can do to support mathematical learning. She maps the terrain of mathematics for young children, exploring different domains of knowledge and linking them to materials, instructional strategies, and dispositions that have the potential to enrich mathematics understanding. Key to this process is her ability to show how play-based teaching is not merely a matter of preparing the environment and stepping back, nor is it a teacher performing as an adult with knowledge. Instead, play-based teaching and learning requires careful preparation of the environment that respects children's autonomy while supporting their discovery of new learning contexts. It also identifies the situations that require the deft hand of a more-competent learner to stretch a child into her zone of proximal development, or when structured instruction might catalyze new and different interactions.

And she does all of this in a way that makes you think, "Wow, this was here the whole time and I didn't even see it." It makes early mathematics real, doable, and relevant, even for the most math phobic among us. It can be the antidote for teachers who struggle to justify their commitment to play. And it will make you look taller and 10 pounds lighter. Well, the last one isn't true, but it represents a wonderful example of Vygotsky's idea that "in play a child always behaves beyond his average age, above his daily behavior; in play it is as though he were a head taller than himself" (1978, p. 102). In our always-wanting-to-get-ahead world, a mode of instruction that gets the student to work above his average should be compelling. The metaphor holds for teachers as well, with play providing opportunities to learn about their students that are outside of the ordinary.

Exploring Mathematics Through Play in the Early Childhood Classroom is one of those books that I wish I had written. It is smart, readable, relevant, and authentically focused on children. Thanks Amy Parks. We're all going to be taller because of you.

—Elizabeth Graue

Part I

CREATING TIME AND SPACE FOR PLAY

CHAPTER 1

Introduction

My first job interview as a prospective teacher was for a position teaching 3rd grade at a K–5 school. Thinking to highlight the progressive pedagogies I'd learned in college, I talked in great depth about my ideas for including science centers, the arts, and block play in the daily curriculum. After listening for a minute or two, the principal held up his hand to silence me.

"Look," he said. "That all sounds great, and if I was looking for a kindergarten teacher, I'd be interested. But every school has a grade where the fun stops, and here, it's 3rd grade."

At the time, I was outraged, but now, remembering this story after nearly 20 years in early childhood education, I find myself wishing that more principals today shared my interviewer's philosophy. Nowadays, fun doesn't even *start* at many elementary schools, and it certainly doesn't wait until 3rd grade to stop.

In our age of standards, tests, schedules, formal observations, scripted curricula, and checklists, many teachers feel that play is a luxury they cannot afford in their classrooms, particularly in schools that serve historically marginalized students—where testing pressure is often highest.

While doll corners, sand tables, and building blocks used to be common tools in early mathematics education, now even 4-year-olds are increasingly engaged with formal assessments of their academic performance in reading and mathematics (Graue, 2006; Miller & Almon, 2009). As Gullo and Hughes write, "The emphasis has become content-oriented, skill-based instruction and learning that teachers assess using conventional measures. Worksheets and other paper and pencil teacher-made tests have become customary practice for determining what specific skills and knowledge children have acquired" (2011, p. 324). In studies commissioned by the Alliance for Childhood, researchers found that kindergarten teachers in New York and Los Angeles reported spending 2 to 3 hours daily on literacy, mathematics, and test preparation and less than 30 minutes each day on "choice" activities, and in Los Angeles a quarter of teachers said there was no time at all for play in their classrooms (Miller & Almon, 2009). In addition, many teachers also know that too many of their students are stressed, miserable, and failing to meet the academic expectations set for them.

This book is for teachers caught in the tension between meeting increasingly high expectations for children's mathematical performances and providing children with humane and happy spaces in which to learn and grow. My goal is to provide you with concrete strategies to foster play, recognize mathematics in play, and design formal lessons that build on children's explorations during play.

One misconception that many have is that providing time for play is in opposition to new expectations that even the youngest children reason abstractly and solve mathematical problems. In truth, much more than in typical lessons, play offers students opportunities to solve nonroutine problems, to persevere, and to make connections among mathematical ideas.

Consider the following interaction from a public school preschool classroom that serves predominantly low-income and minority children: During choice time, Cliff and Ivan return to the block corner, where they play 2 to 3 days a week. On this day, they work together to fill a large square Dulpo board with blocks (see Photo 1.1). In the beginning, pieces go on quickly; however, after not too much time, only a few oddly shaped spaces are left open. Ivan, realizing that it will be difficult to fit in any additional blocks on the first level, begins to build upward; however, Cliff stops him, saying: "No, I'm doing something here." Cliff removes Ivan's tower and then chooses a narrow rectangle and rotates it to fill an

Photo 1.1. Cliff and Ivan Work to Fill in a Large Square with Lego Blocks

open space. He then looks up at Ivan, who is watching, and asks if he wants to help. Ivan agrees, and after watching Cliff for another minute, Ivan removes a block along the perimeter and repositions it so he can place a block in the newly enlarged space.

Now, take a moment to think about the following questions:

1. What makes Cliff and Ivan's interaction play? In other words, how was this engagement different from the other sorts of activities in which students routinely engage during school?
2. Where is the mathematics in this play (if any)?
3. Why might it be important for Cliff and Ivan to encounter this mathematics during play rather than only in formal lessons?

The rest of this introduction discusses these questions in some depth before briefly outlining the rest of the book.

WHAT IS PLAY? OR DO YOU KNOW IT WHEN YOU SEE IT?

On the surface, it may seem unnecessary or even ridiculous to spend any time defining *play*; however, in working with classroom teachers and administrators I have found that a surprisingly wide range of activities are claimed as play. For example, all of the following have been described to me as play:

- Using teddy bear graham crackers to make a graph during a lesson
- Playing kickball in PE
- Painting in Art
- Acting out stories as part of Writer's Workshop
- Playing "Go Fish" and other card games in math class

All of the above activities are probably enjoyable for many children, actively engage their minds and bodies, and promote learning; however, none of those activities would be considered play, according to most definitions, because none of the activities were freely chosen by the children involved. Although there is some disagreement about how precisely to define play, almost all researchers agree that an activity must be voluntary in order to be considered play.

For example, Lifter and Bloom write that play "consists of spontaneous, naturally occurring activities with objects that engage attention and interest" (1998, p. 164). Burghardt (2011) offered five criteria for recognizing and defining play in both people and animals. He wrote that play is spontaneous or pleasurable, functional, different from similar serious behaviors, repeated, and initiated in the absence of stress. Again and again, researchers emphasize similar qualities in play, calling it voluntary, pleasurable, and varied.

These definitions highlight an important quality in Cliff and Ivan's interaction that may not have been immediately apparent. It occurred during choice time. In this preschool classroom, students had about 45 minutes each day when they could choose to engage with a variety of materials, including Lego and wooden blocks, art supplies, dolls, puzzles, kitchen toys, and cars. Furthermore, they could choose how long to spend with any material and with whom to work. Unlike fun activities during formal lessons, they had the power to choose the task, the materials, their companions, and the goal.

This opportunity to make choices is critical. In part, Cliff and Ivan persevered to finish a difficult task because it was *their* difficult task. Cliff, in particular, demonstrated a commitment to completing the task that he had set out and not adapting it because it became challenging. In addition, unlike many school tasks, even those that appear pleasurable, Cliff and Ivan's goal was not simply to be done with the task as quickly as they could so they could go on to the next activity set by the teacher. Because their time was their own to spend, they could be fully in the moment with the task. Even when they disagreed about the goal of the activity, Ivan remained engaged, trying to determine Cliff's agenda, and Cliff invited Ivan to play again after correcting him. Neither of them ended the activity as a result of the disagreement or as a result of its increasing difficulty; nor did they call on a teacher to mediate their disagreement.

Other characteristics of play evident in Cliff and Ivan's interaction—but not in many of the activities in the bulleted list—are the repeated nature of the play and the absence of stress. Although, as far as I know, Cliff and Ivan had never before worked together to fill a square mat, both boys had played with blocks many times before the episode described above. By playing with blocks routinely over the course of the year, the boys built competencies with the materials and developed more complicated play scenarios. So, for example, when Cliff set a task like trying to entirely fill a blank square, he and Ivan could draw on mental images of various sized blocks to successfully complete the task. Similarly, other children began the year by primarily building towers, but by the end of the year would create enclosures and models of other objects, such as cars and airplanes. In his popular book, *The Power of Play*, David Elkind (2007) says that repeated experiences with materials are essential to developing creativity and also to learning perseverance. He argues that when children move rapidly from toy to toy, they do not have the opportunity to explore all the possibilities a material offers or to invent solutions to their own boredom.

With the possible exception of acting out stories during Writing Working, many of the activities in the bulleted list occur only over short periods of time. In PE, the class moves on from kickball to soccer. In Art, the lessons go from painting to sculpting, and in math, graphing and counting lessons are replaced by geometry and measurement. This variation exposes children to many new ideas, but does not allow them to deeply explore all of the possibilities present in a given material. In fact, it is often when children are bored with a frequently used toy that they make a new discovery about how it can be used.

Choice and repetition go hand in hand. When children are allowed to make choices about how to spend their time, not only do they choose activities that they find pleasurable, but they also have opportunities to develop richer understandings over time, provided that the materials are complex enough to support such deep explorations. Similarly, the knowledge that the materials can be returned to again and again removes stress from the situation. Not only is the task at hand not being set or assessed by an adult, but also there is no risk of not getting to finish or not being able to do all that one wants with the materials. Cliff and Ivan can persevere with filling the board today, in part because they know that tomorrow, if they want to build airplanes, they can do that too.

Finally, in addition to considering the qualities that must be present for an interaction to be classified as play, it is also worth considering a few qualities that may be present, but are not essential. For example, the interaction between Cliff and Ivan is an example of social play; however, play can also occur with just one child. In fact, both Cliff and Ivan spent significant amounts of time during their preschool year playing in the block corner independently. This time allowed them to experiment with their own ideas, and also take a break from the continuous social interaction of the busy preschool classroom.

Some people might assume that only interactions that do not involve adults can be considered play; however, this is also not the case. Although in play, children must be free to make choices about what they do and how they do it, adults can participate in a playful manner. That is, by following children's leads rather than by dictating terms. In fact, in Ivan and Cliff's classroom, the teaching assistant in particular was frequently drawn in to play by the children, who would ask her to take on roles in make-believe scenarios or to contribute to a structure they were creating. In fact, adults can make children's play deeper and more meaningful if they intervene carefully. For example, one study found that when adults talked to children about their block structures, children built more complex structures (Gregory, Kim, & Whiren, 2003).

Cliff and Ivan's play provides an example of one kind of play, often called construction play, which supports the learning of mathematics. However, there are many other types of play as well, including pretend play, rough-and-tumble play, rule-based play, and play with the arts (Burghardt, 2011). All of these kinds of play provide some sort of benefit to children in their growth and development.

WHERE'S THE MATH?

Hopefully, you are now convinced that Cliff and Ivan's interaction was different in important ways from other enjoyable experiences that occurred in school, but you may still be wondering about the relationship of their play to the learning of mathematics. After all, neither boy used any mathematical vocabulary in their time together. They did not identify shapes or count—two common mathematical expectations for young children in mathematics. They did not even sort the blocks by shape or color.

Even so, important mathematical learning happens during block play. Broadly, recent research has demonstrated that complex block play in the early years can positively impact spatial reasoning on standardized tests years later (Wolfgang, Stannard, & Jones, 2003). More particularly, we can see direct connections between play like Ivan and Cliff's and the mathematics children are expected to learn in the new Common Core State Standards (National Governors Association Center for Best Practices, 2010).

These new K–12 standards, which currently have been adopted by nearly all U.S. states, name both content and practices that children must learn. The mathematical practices, which are the same in all grades and shown in Figure 1.1, are both habits and ways of thinking necessary to being successful in mathematics. Play can be an important context for children to develop these ways of thinking. For example, when Cliff rejected Ivan's tower, he modeled persevering to solve a problem and as a result Ivan re-engaged with a challenging task. Together, they were able to successfully fill the square and therefore learn that even if a task seems difficult, it can be completed.

The task of fitting in blocks to fill exactly a given space also encouraged the boys to attend to precision. As they worked together to ensure that all of the board was filled and that none of the small pieces hung over the edges, they had to think about which blocks would fit perfectly. Although play, this was not a task where close enough was good enough.

Similarly, the boys had to use their available tools strategically. For example, when Ivan removed a block to create a larger hole, he had to think about the sizes of the available blocks and create a space where one would fit exactly. Early on, when the boys simply snapped blocks onto the board, no strategic thinking was involved. However, as the task neared completion more and more planning was required, along with comparison between the spaces that needed to be filled and the available blocks.

Like this task, play settings often provide children with far more genuine opportunities to engage in these mathematical practices than in formal lessons. Because in lessons, teachers have clear goals about what they want students to do and understand, they are able to nudge students in subtle and obvious ways to complete the task. ("Ivan, why don't you see if you can make the smaller rectangle fit?") In providing these

Figure 1.1. Common Core State Standards for Mathematical Practice

MP1: Make sense of problems and persevere in solving them.

MP2: Reason abstractly and quantitatively.

MP3: Construct viable arguments and critique the reasoning of others.

MP4: Model with mathematics.

MP5: Use appropriate tools strategically.

MP6: Attend to precision.

MP7: Look for and make use of structure.

MP8: Look for and express regularity in repeated reasoning.

hints, teachers often take over a good deal of the mathematical reasoning, while also cutting down on children's opportunities to persevere on their own. Because teachers are (legitimately) concerned with classroom management during formal lessons, they frequently do not want to allow students to become bored and thus to experiment to find their way out of a problem. Play provides a space where children can take lots of time to engage in mathematical practices, without teachers becoming anxious about their ability to stay on task or to complete an assignment at roughly the same time as others.

In addition to opportunities to engage with the mathematical practices, play like Cliff and Ivan's block task also provides opportunities to engage with particular mathematical content. For the primary grades, the new Common Core State Standards emphasize number and operations, but also include standards for geometry, measurement, data, and algebraic reasoning.

Cliff and Ivan's block play most closely relates to standards in geometry. In kindergarten, children will be expected to "describe their physical world using geometric ideas (e.g., shape, orientation, spatial relations) and vocabulary" and "use basic shapes and spatial reasoning to model objects in their environment and to construct more complex shapes" (www.corestandards.org, p. 9).

Cliff and Ivan's play required that they notice and work with the properties of particular shapes (in this case, rectangular prisms). They needed to note which ones were longer or shorter, wider and skinnier. In addition they needed to recognize when rotating a block was necessary to fill a space. These experiences will provide a rich knowledge base later as Cliff and Ivan work with representations of 2-D and 3-D shapes on the printed page and as they solve problems involving rotation and orientation.

More broadly, Cliff and Ivan's play allowed them both opportunities to develop symbolic thinking, which is vital for future work in mathematics (Vygotsky, 1962; Piaget, 1962). Activities like building with blocks, emptying containers, and representing the world through artistic representations allow children to develop ideas related to quantity, comparison, and composition and decomposition of shapes (Lakoff & Núñez, 2000). In addition, the pleasure children find in these play activities is a critical motivator in inspiring children to engage in the work needed to move from one developmental level to the next. As children become tired of a particular kind of play (often as a result of becoming skillful), their desire for new experiences inspires them to engage in more demanding play (Vygotsky, 1962). Adults can support children in deepening the quality of their play.

From this perspective, the role of adults in deepening and extending play is quite important. Although Cliff and Ivan's work provides an important context for developing mathematical ways of thinking and content knowledge, it is important to recognize that this sort of play is not the same as learning mathematics content. In other words, Cliff and Ivan will need to learn to put words to their experiences with the blocks and to generalize beyond the particular task. The learning of both mathematical vocabulary and of creating abstractions (big ideas) from particular experiences is an important role played by formal mathematics lessons. To elaborate, Cliff and Ivan will need to learn, among other things, that a block is called a rectangular prism, that it shares particular features with other rectangular prisms in the world (8 corners, 6 faces, etc.), and that 3-D figures, such as rectangular prisms, can be represented in 2-D on the printed page (but should still call to mind the actual 3-D figure).

We make a mistake if we assume that by playing with toys like blocks, Cliff and Ivan will learn these things automatically. However, we also make a mistake if we do not give Cliff and Ivan the opportunity to develop rich experience bases on their own before intervening as teachers. This is the challenge addressed throughout the rest of this book—figuring out how to provide ample time and productive materials for children to engage in open, exploratory play *and* how to design formal lessons that fully take advantage of the mathematics children have already uncovered during their play.

The following chapter provides strategies for recognizing and drawing on the mathematical play in which children engage outside of the classroom, while Chapter 3 offers ideas for organizing time and space in the classroom for productive play.

Chapters 4 through 7 make connections between the mathematics described in the new Common Core State Standards and common play contexts in early childhood classrooms. The final two chapters before the conclusion look at ways that formal lessons and assessments can be designed to build on children's experiences during play.

CHAPTER 2

Finding Out About Children's Mathematical Play in Multiple Contexts

Recently, I showed a 1st-grade teacher video clips of children from her classroom playing on a seesaw on the playground during the previous year. The children jumped on and off either end of the seesaw as it swayed, trying to get the board to balance just right. When they succeeded, they all hovered off the ground for a moment or two. After looking at the video, the teacher said, "I wish I had known about this. I would have used it when I introduced addition." In looking at the children's play, the teacher realized how the seesaw could become a metaphor for the equals sign that children could understand physically as well as cognitively. In order to balance, the weight on both sides of the seesaw had to be the same. This idea of the equals sign—as meaning "the same as" rather than "write the answer here"—is actually very important to the understanding of equations that needs to be in place for students to reason algebraically. However, because most elementary school children develop their understanding of equals signs through solving written addition, multiplication, subtraction, and division problems, most children tend to see the equals sign as signaling the need to take an action (i.e., "write the answer here") rather than as a statement of equality.

In their research about the ways that people build mathematical understandings through their physical engagements in the world, Lakoff and Núñez (2000) have demonstrated that through interacting with everyday materials, such as containers, collections of small objects, lines, and sticks, children build their conceptions of what mathematics is. For example, Lakoff and Núñez argue that play with containers builds metaphors that later help children to understand the concept of classification.

For example, the number 2 can be conceptualized as being within the container of even numbers, while the number 3 is not. For centuries now, scholars, including thinkers such as Pestalozzi, Friederich Froebel, and Maria Montessori, have recognized the role that physical objects and toys play in children's development of mathematical thinking (Wager & Parks, 2014).

Current research has demonstrated that across demographic groups, all children engage in a wide variety of mathematical play at home and during free time at school. In a study of mathematical play at a preschool, Seo and Ginsburg (2004) found that 88% of children engaged in some kind of mathematical play, including making patterns with beads, building with blocks, and counting and comparing objects. In looking at homes, Tudge and Doucet (2004) found that many children engaged in mathematical play in their homes, with no differences related to race or class. Paying attention to play outside of the classroom can help teachers to recognize where children develop their metaphors for thinking about mathematics and to identify experiences that could be drawn on in the classroom to illustrate difficult concepts. The goal of this chapter is to provide some strategies for linking mathematical play outside of school to what goes on in the classroom.

INVESTIGATING OPPORTUNITIES
FOR MATHEMATICAL PLAY AT SCHOOL

As in the story that opened this chapter, many of the play experiences that relate to mathematics occur outside of the classroom, particularly as children grow older and opportunities for play within the classroom are greatly reduced. Observing your children's school day with mathematical eyes can allow you to build connections between these experiences and the children's learning in the classroom.

The equipment on playgrounds not only provides opportunities for children to build metaphors for, and embodied understandings of, a wide variety of mathematical concepts; but also provides sites where teachers can explicitly invite students to explore particular concepts. These explorations can be done as part of lessons—providing students with an opportunity to move and stretch—or as part of recess with teachers prompting children to engage in a particular activity for a short period of time during their free play. Figure 2.1 is a chart listing some common

Figure 2.1. Mathematics on the Playground

Equipment	Kinds of Play	Mathematical Concepts
Balance Beam	Walking along a line	Building a sense of a number line
	Balancing with arms out	Building a sense of balance or equality, important for understanding equations and balance scales
	Taking big and small steps to cover a distance	
		Understanding the attribute of length
		Understanding that units matter when measuring
Play Structures	Moving to different places	Developing spatial sense
		Practicing directional language (up, down, above, below, etc.)
	Pretending structure is something else (house, airplane, etc.)	Using symbolic thinking
Sandbox	Emptying and filling containers	Building metaphors for classification
		Understanding attribute of volume
	Building structures	
Seesaw	Balancing	Building a sense of equality
	Going up and down	Understanding the attribute of weight
		Developing an understanding of a balance scale
Swings	Swinging	Comparing and naming attributes (higher, faster, farther, etc.)

playground equipment and the mathematical concepts that can emerge for children during play.

In addition to play with equipment, children may also develop spatial relationships through games like hide-and-seek, when they have to picture playground structures and imagine where other children might be, or through tag, when they have to make judgments about who is near and who is far, how fast each person can move, and where each person is likely to go next. Games with jump ropes can develop counting and patterning through repetition and rhythmic chants. In all of these cases, the point is not that children will master these mathematical concepts through play, but that they develop ways of understanding the world that they will bring to their engagements with mathematics and that teachers can leverage consciously when discussing new concepts.

CONDUCTING A COMMUNITY SURVEY

Of course children play not only on the playground attached to the school, but also in a variety of sites throughout their neighborhood. Exploring the neighborhood in which your children live can help you develop connections with children and their families broadly, but exploring with an eye toward mathematics can provide you with additional ways of connecting your children's play in informal environments with formal mathematics lessons in the classroom. For example, when a group of prospective teachers began to investigate the neighborhood around their placement school, they found that there was a small neighborhood store that many of the children visited regularly while playing to buy snacks and candy. Their observations demonstrated that many of the children engaged in some relatively complicated mathematics during these visits, including making judgments about what they could afford individually, and if they pooled their money, and how any purchases should be fairly shared based on the money collected from each person. By drawing on this context in the classroom, the prospective teachers were able to design word problems that they knew the students could use their personal experiences to solve.

Try conducting an investigation of the opportunities for mathematical play in your school's community. This might include identifying playgrounds other than the one at your school, in particular paying attention to features that are different from the equipment your children have access to during recess. You might also visit a few places that families might frequent on the weekends to identify experiences that you could mathematize for kids. Places with sites for mathematical learning could include libraries, public gardens and zoos, museums, and bowling alleys. Often teachers and curricula attempt to make connections with "real-world" contexts in mathematics problems, but too often these contexts are as unfamiliar to children as the mathematics being presented. For example, problems may be based on circuses, amusement parks, or horseback riding, when no child in the classroom has ever experienced any of these things. The goal of investigating the community for sites of mathematical play is to identify contexts that children actually understand so that connections made will be meaningful to them. In addition, you may be able to expand what parents know about recreation opportunities in the community. For example, many parents visit public libraries regularly, but may not understand how stopping to play with the puzzles or blocks provided could be just as important for their children as checking out books. Similarly, you can alert parents to mathematical opportunities in common recreation sites that they may not have previously considered, such as free play groups in libraries or museums.

REACHING OUT TO FAMILIES

Of course much of children's play—mathematical and otherwise—occurs in children's homes. If teachers can find out about the play children routinely engage in regularly, they can leverage those experiences in their daily teaching, ensure that the classroom contains materials that children may not have access to during play at home, and can support parents in promoting mathematical play at home. For example, in working with a rural school that served primarily low-income families, I was surprised to learn that most of the children had access to technology in their homes, either through tablets, their parents' phones, or through game systems that connected to televisions. However, only one of the families I visited had a comprehensive set of blocks in the home. Without exploring the families' resources, I might have assumed that these children did not have access to technology out of school and could have thought that an important role for the school would be to provide these children with significant time to engage with computers and other technology. Although the "digital divide," is a real concern (Purcell, Heaps, Buchanan, & Friedrich, 2013), in this community access to blocks and puzzles was a bigger issue for the youngest children. One parent explained that because sets of blocks were so expensive, it made more sense to buy a tablet, which she imagined her children could use throughout their schooling instead of just in their early childhood. Another parent said that because cable was so expensive, it made more sense to have a DVD player and a tablet with games on it to amuse children. Given this particular context, it made much more sense for teachers in the early grades to provide ample time and materials for block play during the school day than to focus on getting children access to screen time. In addition, learning about the play materials children had in their homes caused us to think about ways to get materials that promote mathematical play into homes.

As a researcher, I was able to make time to conduct home visits with many families, which allowed me to see the kinds of play opportunities for children firsthand. Of course, teachers can also make these kinds of visits, which offer opportunities to learn not just about children's play experiences, but also their families, their parents' work lives, their weekly routines, their neighborhoods, and learning resources (Kyle, McIntyre, Miller, & Moore, 2002). Many teachers have reported that these kinds of visits not only provide productive insights for planning lessons, but also that they have significantly changed the relationships they have with their children and their families. That was certainly my experience as a classroom teacher. If you are interested in home visits, you can incorporate questions about play into your visit. The book, *Reaching Out: A K–8 Resource for Connecting Families and Schools* (Kyle, McIntyre, Miller, & Moore, 2002), offers many helpful suggestions for getting started.

However, if you don't yet feel you have the time or the inclination to do home visits, you can still find out about children's play experiences at home by conducting a play survey. Figure 2.2 is one sample, but you could tailor it for your context.

Although young children may not be able to respond to surveys on their own, they can also report on their play at home. A show-and-tell activity could provide an opportunity for students to bring in a favorite toy and talk about how they use it. Students could also draw pictures of them playing at home to discuss in small groups, or, if your school has resources, disposable cameras or inexpensive digital cameras could be sent home to record play.

In responding to surveys, you can make two moves as a teacher. The first is to identify play experiences that could be leveraged during formal mathematics lessons. Often when teachers attempt to connect mathematics to the real world, they draw on experiences from their own lives, such as cooking, shopping, or sewing. However, these activities may mean little to children; whereas, experiences rolling a dice and moving on a game board, playing a video game where you try to accumulate points or objects, or playing a group game like tag could all provide contexts for imagining problems related to quantity, to more and less, and to addition and subtraction. Contexts and understandings students already have can provide a manageable entry point to new math concepts for children. In addition, drawing contexts identified in play surveys can position children in the classroom as experts about something—such as a particular game—which allows them to build confidence in their own abilities.

Figure 2.2. Play Survey

Dear Families,

Young children learn a lot through play. I would like to know more about how your children play so I can make connections between their play and our lessons in the classroom. Please answer the questions below and return this paper to me. Thanks!

Child's Name: _____

Adult Completing Survey: _____

1. What are your child's favorite toys? How does he or she play with them?

2. What did your child like to play with when he or she was little?

3. What does your child like to do outside?

4. Does your child play at any playgrounds? Which ones? What does he or she like to do?

5. What games does your child like to play? (For example: board games, games with other children, video games, games on a tablet or other electronic device)

6. Does your child ever play with blocks or puzzles? What does he or she do?

In addition to drawing on experiences children do have in their homes, play surveys can also allow you to identify play contexts that children may not be familiar with, but which are known to support mathematical development. This concern is what prompted our questions about puzzle and block play. Research shows these two kinds of play have a significant impact on children's later spatial reasoning, so ensuring that children have these opportunities makes sense (e.g., Levine, Ratliff, Huttenlocher, & Cannon, 2012; Wolfgang, Stannard, & Jones, 2003). If children do not have these materials in their homes, then teachers can provide time and materials at school. If children do have these materials, teachers may be able to send home ideas for parents on how to scaffold the play in more mathematical plays. (Many of these ideas are discussed in Chapter 4.)

In addition, teachers can send home activities specifically designed to promote mathematical play. For example, teachers can send home kits that contain a recipe for play dough and the necessary ingredients (see Figure 2.3).

Figure 2.3. Play Dough Instructions

MAKING PLAY DOUGH!

1. Use the recipe below and the ingredients and tools sent home to make a batch of play dough with your child.

2. Allow your child to play with the play dough for a while. Don't worry about doing anything special. We are interested in how children play at home. Use the camera to take pictures of what your child creates.

3. Turn off the recorder when finished and send back to school with the camera.

PLAY DOUGH RECIPE

Measure into a small pan:

    1 cup flour
    ½ cup salt
    2 teaspoons cream of tartar

Add:

    1 tablespoon baby oil
    1 cup water with 6–10 drops of food coloring added

Cook over medium-high heat. At first it may seem like too much water, but it will boil off and turn solid in about 3 minutes. ALLOW IT TO COOL. Then you and your child can knead smooth and play!

An activity like this encourages a variety of mathematical thinking, including comparing length and size, measuring volume and length, and counting. In addition, it prompts the use of mathematical vocabulary such as longer, shorter, bigger, cup, teaspoon, and half in a meaningful context. Photo 2.1 shows a child following the play dough recipe with the help of her older sister.

In my experience activities like these also tend to involve more children in the family in the activity, increasing the mathematical impact. One parent who participated in this play dough activity said that she had never made play dough at home before, but now her son wanted to do it frequently.

Teachers can also create backpacks with mathematical toys and send them home for play. For example, sets of Lego blocks are relatively small and light. These can be sent home along with pictures of possible structures for children to build. The pictures are often included in Lego kits but they can also be taken by the teacher. As with the play dough activity, play with Lego blocks prompts a number of mathematical skills, including composing and decomposing 3-dimensional shapes, moving between 2-dimensional representations and 3-dimensional objects, comparing size and length, and discovering relationships between different sized blocks. If resources are available, cameras can be included in the backpacks so that children can take pictures of their creations. These pictures then

Photo 2.1. An Older Sibling Helps Her Sister Measure for the Play Dough Recipe

provide new mathematical opportunities in the classroom, where children can use mathematical language to describe what they made and can use the pictures of others as models for their own building in the classroom. Photos 2.2 and 2.3 show children playing at home with Lego

Photo 2.2. Blake Uses Available Blocks to Build a Car

Photo 2.3. Girls Refer to a Diagram to Help Build Their Lego House

kits. The pictures in the kits allowed the children to practice interpreting a 2-dimensional image in order to create a 3-D structure.

In addition to blocks, math backpacks can also be used to share puzzles and board games, encouraging a variety of mathematical play throughout the year. Because play is so intimately connected to both children's home lives and to their early mathematical learning, investigations such as those described above provide an invaluable opportunity to strengthen bonds between homes and schools and to support a pleasurable entry into early mathematics.

CHAPTER 3

Organizing Time and Space at School for Mathematical Play

Often, even teachers who are committed to learning through play find it difficult to make time for children's independent exploration of materials, particularly given the many constraints imposed on their days by school or district mandates. Securing administrative support for choice or center time will be key, and may require conversations with your administrators. This is especially true in elementary schools that serve older children because administrators may not have backgrounds in early childhood education. The book *Developmentally Appropriate Practice in Early Childhood Programs* produced by the National Association for the Education of Young Children (Copple & Bredekamp, 2009) could be a useful tool for structuring these conversations because it lays out best practices for early childhood classrooms in ways that are clear and easy to understand. The book takes the position that it is vital for children to have "significant periods of time in which they choose what they want to do and, together with other children, direct their own activities" (Copple & Bredekamp, 2009, p. 40). Other resources for approaching these conversations with administrators are included in Chapter 10.

ORGANIZING TIME

Once you have support for a regular center time, you can begin to think about when you would like to incorporate it and what your expectations for children's participation might be. In preschool or kindergarten, where choice time is most likely to be an expected part of the day, centers might include a wide range of choices, such as imaginative play settings like kitchens and doctor's offices, literacy play materials such as puppets or writing tools, and mathematics play materials, such as blocks and puzzles. While this structure provides the maximum amount of freedom and choice for children, from a mathematical perspective, it also presents some challenges. Many children return to the same centers again and again and, therefore, may never engage with the materials most likely to promote mathematical thinking and learning.

One way to address this challenge might be to have some days of the week where children can choose only among the centers likely to promote mathematical thinking. These will be discussed in more detail throughout the book, but they might include: blocks, puzzles, measuring tools, games, counters, dolls, and play dough. If you have time, another possibility might be to have an open choice time during the day as well as a more focused choice time, where the open centers rotate between those focused on mathematics and literacy. Whatever the structure, the goal is to create a time when all children can engage with materials likely to promote mathematical thinking.

Finding time for this in Grades 1–2, where center time is no longer taken for granted, can be an even greater challenge. Beginning in a small way can be helpful, such as using half of your math time 2 or 3 days a week for free choice math centers. These centers can also be made available at the beginning of the day or at the end of the day, as alternatives to seat work. Finding the time for these engagements may require an honest assessment of your day, examining how you are spending your time and really reflecting on the benefits that students get from various activities. In observing many early childhood classrooms, I have found that practices like morning work, viewing videos, and other interactive white board activities, and extended whole-class activities like calendar time often take up significant amounts of the day without deeply engaging children. As an example, activities at an interactive white board, when done as a whole class, allow only a small number of children to participate. Most need to sit quietly and watch while one or two children interact with the board. However, if the interactive white board were available as a center, all children could not only interact with the board but could spend the time actively engaged with other materials, rather than watching their classmates. Similarly, if you show one video a week, you might ask yourself whether that time could be better used for choice time. Even if you are only able to set aside a half an hour each Friday, that time can be valuable. Don't let the perfect be the enemy of the good. Even providing your children with a little time each week to engage in mathematical play can support their development as learners.

HELPFUL MATERIALS

Fortunately, given the emphasis on the use of manipulatives in mathematics, most schools have many materials that can be used for mathematical play. The ways that these materials are displayed and organized can in themselves promote mathematical learning. Many of the materials listed in this section will be discussed in more depth in later chapters. The goal here is to provide a quick checklist of materials that might be useful, as well as suggestions for how to organize materials in ways likely to promote mathematical thinking.

Blocks

Many preschool and kindergarten classrooms will have wooden blocks included in their standard set of classroom materials. Throughout the year, all blocks should be available to children to build with; however, materials can be added to scaffold more complex play as the year goes on, including sets of families or animals, pictures of structures to build, or vehicles. Classrooms may also have small brick blocks, such as Lego blocks. These blocks allow children to make different kinds of structures and are particularly useful for exploring the ways that equivalent lengths can be made from different blocks. Brick blocks are also a good choice for the older grades, because they take up less space for storage and during play. Although brand-name Lego blocks can be expensive, many teacher supply companies have generic sets of brick blocks with more than 1,000 blocks available for purchase for less than $100. If you have instructional money available, magnetic tiles also make fabulous building materials that tend to be very attractive to children. These tiles, which are made by a number of companies, allow children to create 3-D structures using various squares and triangles. In addition to being attractive for play, they are also useful materials for building geometric figures for math lessons, such as cubes, rectangular prisms, and pyramids.

Puzzles

In building a puzzle collection, it is important to think about scaffolding more advanced thinking over time. The easiest puzzles have large pieces, often with handles, that fit into single holes. More complex puzzles form pictures that need to be fit together. Both the number of pieces and the complexity of the picture contribute to difficulty. Over the course of the year, the puzzles available to children should increase in difficulty. Once children begin to complete puzzles from memory, those puzzles should be retired and replaced with more challenging ones. Some puzzles will have the completed picture underneath the pieces or on the cover of the box; however, if your puzzles do not have these, it can be helpful to make pictures of the completed puzzles available for children to rely on. Pattern block puzzles can also be productive for children. These are useful because most classrooms have sets of pattern blocks already. Templates for various puzzles can be downloaded for free from the Internet by searching for "pattern block templates." Like other puzzles, pattern block templates should be scaffolded for difficulty, with templates with defined shapes and colors being available first, then defined shapes without colors, then outlines of larger figures without lines marking the individual shapes.

Object Collections

Buckets of colorful materials invite children to count, sort, and compare as well as to engage in imaginative play. These materials could come from sets of standard mathematics manipulatives, such as bears and dinosaurs, or from found objects gathered by the children, such as pennies, keys, or shells. Ideally, materials would be rotated regularly to maintain interest.

Measuring Tools

Balances, measuring tapes, measuring cups and spoons, and rulers all invite children to engage with measurement ideas, even before they are ready to formally engage with the concepts. Changing the materials available to measure over time can promote new engagements. For example, one month the balance might be stored in a bucket with plastic farm animals and another month it might be stored with bean bags. Similarly, rulers might be organized next to varyingly sized dolls or stuffed animals or even cutouts of children's feet. Materials useful for measuring volume include buckets of cotton balls, which are noiseless and easy to clean up, or larger pasta shapes, such as wagon wheels or shells (which are easier to clean up than small ones). Pasta can be colored with rubbing alcohol and food coloring by covering the dried pasta with rubbing alcohol and as many drops of food coloring as you like. Allow the pasta to sit overnight, and then drain out the liquid and allow the pasta to dry on a paper towel.

Pretend Play

Many pretend play contexts can support mathematical thinking, including stores, doctor's offices, and kitchens. However, the available materials often need to be tweaked or arranged in ways to make mathematics more salient for children. For example, posting recipes in kitchens such as in Figure 3.1 can encourage children to count. Stickers, stamps or picture cut-outs could be provided so children could construct their own recipes. Similarly, including measuring tapes as part of the supplies for a doctor's office, or a scale for a grocery store can encourage children to engage with mathematics. The key is to think about possible mathematics for various settings and to consider ways that particular materials might elicit these engagements for kids.

Figure 3.1. Fruit Salad Recipe

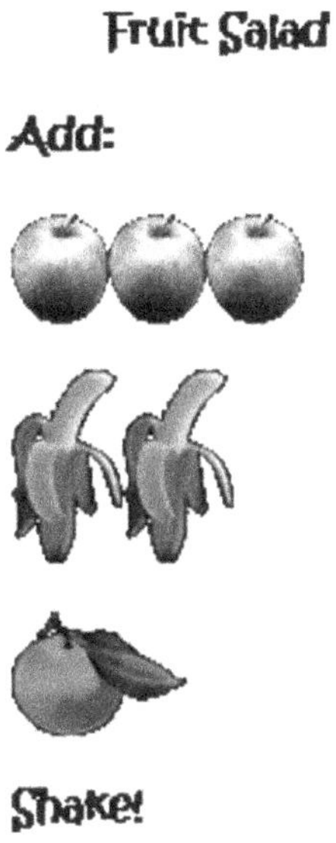

Play Dough

Play dough not only allows children to practice fine motor skills but also tends to lead to a large number of mathematical conversations. While engaging with each other children naturally compare their creations to see who had the longest or the most. When creating large collections of objects children count them to see how many they have. These engagements can be fostered by including number- and shape-based cookie cutters, plastic knives or scissors for cutting objects in half, and pictures of possible creations that encourage students to move from 2-D to 3-D representations.

Games

For independent play, games work best for older children. Because 4-, 5-, and 6-year-olds are still struggling to manage the social interactions that go along with games and the emotions involved in winning and losing, for young children, games to support mathematical learning are often most effective when supported by a teacher or an adult volunteer. However in 2nd and 3rd grade, many children can play games independently. In this case, the challenge becomes choosing games that will allow students to engage with an area of mathematics that is challenging for them. For this purpose, making games used as part of the formal mathematics curricula available during choice time is often a good solution. Children have already been introduced to the rules, and the games have been designed to promote grade-level mathematics. Because you want children to be able to regulate themselves during choice time, it is important to choose games that require very little adult intervention.

STRUCTURING THE DAY

Finding time and materials are important, but they are not enough to highlight mathematical thinking in play. Teachers need to use instructional strategies both to promote mathematical play and to help make mathematical ideas explicit for children. Many early childhood teachers, drawing on curricula like High/Scope, already use a planning time before play and a debriefing time afterward. These times can be used to guide children toward mathematical play. For example, during planning time, you might decide to highlight a material—like measuring tools—that hasn't been used very often, demonstrating some of the activities that children could engage in. Or you might present a problem like wondering about how many dolls you have or which is the largest. Or you might present a challenge for children, such as introducing a new puzzle or putting up a picture of a complicated block structure that students can be encouraged to build. The goal during this time is to both engage children's interest in the mathematical materials and also to push children toward more complex play than they may have engaged in previously.

This can also be a time to push children out of their comfort zone. Although children should have opportunities to make many choices during play, if you notice that a group of children returns to the same center day after day, you might intervene during planning time, by saying that you have noticed this pattern, and suggesting that today the child choose from one of three centers you offer. This is particularly important for children who never engage with the materials most likely to promote mathematical thinking.

Similarly, a debriefing period at the end of choice time each day can provide an opportunity to highlight the mathematical thinking students engaged in that day, to encourage children to learn from one another, and to connect formal mathematical vocabulary and concepts to the play that occurred that day (Seo, 2003). Children can volunteer to discuss what they did during the center time, but teachers can also choose children to highlight if they want to direct class attention toward a particular activity. If the technology is available, digital cameras and interactive white boards can be used to support these conversations. For example, teachers could snap pictures of block structures and ask the child who built them to describe them. Teachers can also describe these structures themselves, using the appropriate mathematical vocabulary to discuss shape, orientation, and quantity. Opportunities to use these words in a meaningful context are important for children to develop a real sense of what the words mean and how to use them. Pictures taken could also be posted or shown on the interactive white board (IWB) the next day to launch a new play session.

A debriefing time can also be an opportunity to talk through a child's problem-solving strategy. For example, if a teacher notices that a child looked at the larger picture of a puzzle to recognize that a blue piece went on the bottom, this can be talked about with or without pictures. This strategy of moving from a whole to a part is important to composing and decomposing figures, a skill highlighted for young children in the Common Core State Standards in Mathematics (CCSSM), which expect children to compose more complex 2-D shapes using simple shapes (K.G.B.6 and 1.G.A.2). (The numbers in the parentheses refer to specific Common Core State Standards. The first letter or number refers to the grade level, while the second letter refers to the content, in this case, geometry.) By naming and describing these strategies, teachers make it possible for other children to use them. In addition, children whose strategies are highlighted begin to develop identities as "math people" as they see their success in activities like solving puzzles or comparing the height of dolls recognized and valued. For that reason, making connections between the informal mathematics that occurs during play and formal mathematics is exceptionally important. When teachers see connections between the current mathematical focus of the classroom and play activities, debriefing time is an opportunity to make that connection explicit for all children. In addition, by giving attention to the mathematical activities that occur during play, teachers demonstrate that they value these activities, making it more likely that other children will choose to participate in them in the future.

In addition to making connections between play and informal mathematics, during debriefing, teachers can also create settings for "playful learning." Most definitions of play rightly emphasize that choices about the length and kinds of engagement are central to real play (Wager & Parks, 2014). From this perspective, activities guided by the teacher to scaffold mathematical learning cannot truly be considered play. However, playful learning engagements can provide some of the fun that children experience during real play, along with opportunities to engage in significant mathematics. Having an adult, whether a teacher, or paraprofessional, or volunteer, lead small-group activities during free choice time can be an important opportunity not only for children to engage in mathematical thinking and learning, but also an opportunity for adults to teach children how to interact with materials in mathematical ways. All of the activities mentioned above, including block building, puzzle play, measuring, and working with play dough can be used during small-group activities. However, unlike engagements during free choice, during these playful learning engagements adults can introduce particular activities for children.

For example, children can be encouraged to build and describe particular structures with blocks, to solve puzzles using particular strategies or at levels that the adult judges are appropriate for the child, or to make collections of various sizes with toys or play dough cut-outs. During these engagements adults can both consciously push children to engage in more complex work or teach strategies that may be useful when children work independently at other times. Moving materials to small-group tables also gives children who have difficulty maintaining possession of attractive toys in the open space of free time the opportunity to have prolonged engagements with toys like blocks or play dough. For example, when observing preschool classrooms, I often notice that a small number of boys tend to dominate the block-playing areas, sometimes even taking blocks from other children's structures. These challenges can make engaging with certain materials less attractive for some children, and they may decide only to work with materials that others do not want. Having an adult available to support engagement gives these students the opportunity to explore without having to defend their space.

These adult-supported activities during free time should not take the place of formal mathematics lessons, whether whole-class or small-group, at other parts of the day. They can enrich the kind of mathematical activity that occurs during center time, and can provide an opportunity for teachers to observe what children can and cannot do in a setting that feels fun and comfortable for the children. For example, there are many toys that encourage counting of sets and identifying numbers. Spending a few days rotating a class through engagements with these materials could take the place of a more formal assessment, allowing teachers to develop a sense of what each child has already mastered, and to make decisions about what to emphasize next. Too often preschool and kindergarten classrooms continue to emphasize rote counting, long after most children have mastered this skill. Assessing competence in an informal setting can provide important information about when it is time to move on while also maintaining children's interest.

Broadly, it is important to recognize that while mathematical learning and engagements can occur during play when children have opportunities to work with meaningful materials, the learning and thinking are far more likely to be appropriate and mathematically significant if the play settings are carefully scaffolded by teachers so that children are doing more and more complex work as the year goes on (Ginsburg, Lee, & Boyd, 2008; Graham, Nash, & Paul, 1997).

Part II

HIGHLIGHTING THE MATHEMATICS IN PLAY

CHAPTER 4

Blocks, Puzzles, and Dolls
The Geometry Standards

Let's begin the focus on geometry by considering a question from the 4th-grade 2011 National Assessment of Educational Progress (see Figure 4.1). Students were asked to identify how many more cubes were used to build Solid A than Solid B.

Nearly half of the 4th-graders tested got this question wrong. Given students' performance on the calculation items on the test, as well as the fact that students were allowed to use a calculator on this question, it is unlikely that subtracting 12 – 8 caused the difficulties. Instead, the challenge almost certainly lay in counting the blocks used to make Solid B because not all of the small cubes are visible. A task like this requires that students recognize 2-dimensional representations of 3-dimensional figures, compare two 3-D figures, and decompose larger shapes into smaller shapes. All of these abilities lay at the heart of both the geometry strand of the Common Core State Standards and constructive play with blocks.

Students also tend to have difficulty on puzzlelike tasks, which require similar geometric understandings. On the 2009 NAEP, only 43% of 4th-graders were able to answer a question that asked them to use

Figure 4.1. Which Figure Has More Cubes?

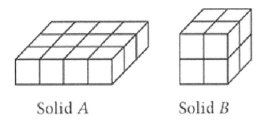

Solid *A*   Solid *B*

two triangles to create a shape that had the following properties: four sides, no overlapping pieces, no parallel sides. Play with both geometric and picture puzzles offers children opportunities to manipulate shapes to create new figures and to discover the impact of rotating and flipping figures. For example, in Photo 4.1, the two children are working together to build a structure that requires they rotate triangles in order to make a seamless side for their building.

Photo 4.1. Children Building with Magnetic Block Tiles

Working with physical objects in the primary grades helps students develop the mental representations that will allow them to work with more abstract representations—such as drawings and written descriptions—later on. Without these experiences, students are forced to rely on half-remembered algorithms for finding the volume of solid objects, or on trying to reason out the construction of such a figure without a physical model. Perhaps more than any other strand in mathematics, deep understandings of geometry in the later years require rich early experiences with physical objects.

BIG IDEAS IN GEOMETRY FOR THE PRIMARY GRADES

For the primary grades, the CCSS divide the geometry standards into three major themes: (1) identifying and describing shapes, (2) analyzing, comparing, creating, and composing shapes, and (3) reasoning with shapes and their attributes. Of course, young students need lots of practice with new vocabulary, but they also need practice rotating and flipping shapes so that they come to see a triangle as a triangle no matter which way it's turned. Children should also learn to identify and to have language for differentiating between 2-D shapes (flat, 2-D, or plane) and 3-D figures (solid, 3-D).

Many of the major ideas in geometry in the primary grades relate to the composing and decomposing of shapes. Composing and decomposing refer to "putting together and taking apart and [apply] to numbers as well as to geometry and measurement" (NRC, 2009, p. 352). Students compose shapes when they put together two triangles to make a square, when they build towers with multiple blocks, and when they construct a design with a variety of different shapes. Students decompose when they recognize that a larger figure can be divided into smaller parts, either by literally taking it apart or by imagining a line that divides the larger figure into pieces. Both of the NAEP questions discussed above require that students either decompose a figure (picture the larger cube as a set of smaller cubes) or compose a figure (place the two triangles together to create a quadrilateral).

Sometimes early grades teachers minimize attention to geometry because most children are able to quickly name a variety of shapes and even key attributes (such as the number of corners). However, more in-depth experiences are needed in order for children to build the capabilities to tackle more difficult experiences later. Composing and decomposing figures (whether through blocks, puzzles, or other toys) provide opportunities for students to identify and analyze key attributes of solid figures, to create larger shapes from smaller ones, and to practice language describing the features and the positions of their creations. The rest of the chapter will explore in more depth the geometric ideas embedded in different play contexts, and will provide suggestions for making that mathematics apparent to children during play as well as adding complexity to children's efforts. The goal in each context for teachers is to help children both build vocabulary to talk about shapes and also to push them toward seeing relationships among shapes that will help them solve problems later.

FACILITATING BLOCK PLAY

A great deal of research has demonstrated that block play supports the geometric thinking and reasoning called for in the CCSS (Casey et al., 2008; NRC, 2009). For example, children who play regularly with sets of wooden blocks show increasingly sophisticated thinking about composition the more time they spend with blocks engaged with tasks such as by combining blocks to made new shapes (Kamii, Miyakawa, & Kato, 2004). For almost 100 years research has demonstrated the importance of children's block play for developing spatial thinking and geometric reasoning (e.g., Casey et al., 2008; Guanella, 1934) as well as for the development of mathematical thinking more broadly (e.g., Caldera et al., 1999). More recent studies have begun to demonstrate relationships between the quantity and quality of children's block play and their performances on tests of spatial reasoning as late as 7th grade (e.g., Wolfgang, Stannard, & Jones, 2001; 2003). Despite this research on the impact block play can have on children's mathematical development, fewer and fewer classrooms have adequate blocks for play or time for children to explore the materials even when they are available (Miller & Almon, 2009). Sets of wooden blocks, Lego, and Dulpo blocks, and even unifix snapping cubes can all provide opportunities for children to explore composing and decomposing shapes and to develop the ability to visualize and describe geometric figures.

Although expensive, wooden block sets provide one of the most durable and flexible tools for promoting early geometric thinking. Photo

Photo 4.2. Block Road with Four Equivalent Sections

4.2 depicts a block road designed by a preschool child. Creating this road provided the child with opportunities to practice composing and decomposing shapes. Each unit of the road is made with different blocks. The decision to do this was a conscious one on the part of the child. He could have made a road that was comprised only of the large rectangles. Similarly, he could have made units that were smaller than the original rectangle. Instead, he chose to work with units that were all identical in area, but composed differently, which provided the opportunity to compose the large rectangle in three different ways. Finally, colored blocks also allow for students to begin to make distinctions between defining attributes of shapes (sides, corners) and nondefining attributes (color, orientation). The ability to make these kinds of distinctions is included as one of the 1st-grade standards in the CCSS.

The more complex structures students make with blocks, the more opportunities they have to explore mathematical relationships. Moving from piles and towers, to enclosed spaces, to 3-D structures with arches and other elaborations, presents new problems for children to consider. For example, as Eliot built a square enclosure, he ran out of large rectangular blocks and switched to smaller square blocks, discovering that two small squares made a unit the size of the larger rectangle. As his building grew in height, he began to use pairs of triangles to create same-sized units. This act of composing new shapes forced Eliot to consider the properties of each different shape and to note the ways that squares and triangles fit together. This activity, like many block-building projects, embedded many of the CCSS within it, including comparing 3-D shapes (K.G.B.4), composing 3-D shapes to create composite shapes (1.G.A.2), and portioning a rectangle into same size squares (2.G.A.2). Because of this, children who have many of these informal building experiences have a rich repertoire of connections to draw on during formal instruction around these topics.

Because Lego blocks connect together, they allow children to create more complex structures more easily. In addition, the flat Lego boards that students can use for building create particular kinds of mathematical problems. In Photo 4.3, Mila creates a rectangle with her Lego blocks. Creating this requires that she makes four sides of equal lengths and that she choose the proper length block pieces to do this correctly. Later, she chose blocks to exactly fill in the empty space in the middle, which provided her with practice composing a large rectangle with many smaller rectangles.

Photo 4.3. Mila Makes an Open Rectangle with Lego Blocks

In addition, more advanced Lego sets often come with diagrams to assist children in making particular projects. Sometimes early childhood teachers are skeptical of these sorts of diagrams because the drawings can reduce opportunities for imagination and creativity on the part of the children. However, mathematically, the diagrams present opportunities for children to learn to move between 2-D and 3-D representations of objects, a skill that is vital for doing geometry in the upper grades (2.G.A.1 and 6.G.A.4). Making these diagrams available to students, but not insisting on their use, is a wonderful opportunity to introduce more possibilities to engage with mathematics.

For example, at a family math night at the school, one station included several boxes of Lego blocks, including special pieces, such as wheels and trees, and written directions for making specific projects. Four-year-old Dahlia came to the event with her mother and her 6-year-old sister, Tamara. Her mother took the written directions for a house, held them in front of Tamara, and quietly talked her through the process of building. As Tamara carefully matched blocks with those in the picture and worked to create an enclosed square, Dahlia began to build a tower with 2-by-8 blocks. Dahlia looked for blocks that were all the same size, rejecting those that were too short or too skinny, but ultimately accepting some that were the correct size, but a different color. Meanwhile, Tamara, having created the floor plan for her building, began to build up the walls on her own, making sure to find blocks that would be exactly the right length. Occasionally, Tamara stopped to look at the diagram and count the rows of blocks to ensure that a door or a window was placed correctly. After watching Tamara for a moment, Dahlia located a window and a door, which she attached next to her tower. She pulled on her mother's sleeve and said "See my house." Her mother looked over, saying, "That's pretty, Dahlia. What you going to do next?"

In this episode, Dahlia, with her mother's help, used Tamara's construction as a model for her own work, while Tamara relied on the provided diagram as a model for her house. In the process, both girls modeled shapes in the real world (K.G.B.5), composed 3-D shapes (1.G.A.2), and recognized shapes with particular attributes (1.G.A.1). This episode also demonstrates the ways that open block play can be easily leveled to meet the needs of various children. While Tamara was able to read a diagram and to build an enclosed structure, Dahlia worked to build a single tower of identical blocks. The written diagram moved Tamara toward more complex play, while Tamara's construction motivated Dahlia. Often in block corners, complex play moves from one child to another with little intervention on the part of teachers.

It is worthwhile to take a moment to consider the relationship between gender and block play. Research over time has shown that boys do tend to express a greater preference for block play than girls do (Kersh, Casey, & Young, 2008); however, work has also shown that when girls engage with block play they build equally complex structures (Caldera et al., 1999) and that, regardless of expressed preference, girls do spend significant time playing with blocks when given the opportunity (Seo & Ginsburg, 2004). One issue that may be important for teachers to consider in relation to block play is whether girls can get their hands on materials. In the preschool classroom I observed, girls often had a hard time moving into the space where blocks were kept and in maintaining control of their materials in response to boys' attempts to gather up all available blocks. Different sorts of organizational structures—such as making blocks available at a rotating center or as part of a table activity supervised by the teacher—may help to support all children in getting their hands on the materials.

Teachers can provide further support for children during open play by asking questions, posing problems, and providing resources that encourage students to make their play more complex. They can also introduce mathematical terms, such as face, edge, triangular, and rectangular, into children's play. A recent study demonstrated that children built more complex structures during block play when nearby adults made leading statements such as "I wonder if you could build a house with four walls" or "Sometimes people use blocks to join structures" (Gregory, Kim, & Whiren, 2003). Paraprofessionals or parent volunteers may be particularly effective in filling these roles since such statements from teachers could be read as commands by the children and might disrupt the process of open play.

Teachers could also pose problems by taking pictures of structures and displaying them either on a bulletin board near the block corner or on an interactive white board before play time. Children might be motivated to create equally complex structures themselves or even to replicate what a classmate did the previous day, which requires a great deal of mathematical thinking. In addition, resources such as laminated copies of Lego diagrams or photos of buildings or bridges might serve as prompts for children in their play, particularly if they are frequently rotated and discussed before playtime begins. Providing paper, crayons, and markers near the block corner (as well as an opportunity to display creations afterward) might encourage students to represent their work, providing important practice in drawing shapes and representing 3-D objects on a 2-D plane. Figure 4.2 provides some teacher comments and questions that can help focus children's geometric thinking during block play.

PRACTICING WITH PUZZLES

Puzzles, both the traditional picture-based ones that are typically found in homes, and the geometric ones based on manipulating pattern blocks, offer important opportunities for children to experiment with and manipulate shapes. In particular, puzzles allow children to recognize shapes despite their orientation and to rotate them to match holes, as well as to practice composing and decomposing figures. A recent study of children's play at home found that children who played with puzzles between 26 and 46 months performed better on a test of spatial skills at 56 months than children who did not have these experiences (Levine, Ratliff, Huttenlocher, & Cannon, 2012). As children work with puzzles, they typically become more skilled at recognizing and manipulating shapes and composing and decomposing figures. Children tend to begin to solve puzzles by using trial and error and progress to using strategies to solve puzzles intentionally (Clements, Wilson, & Sarama, 2004). Picture puzzles and geometric puzzles offer different opportunities for different kinds of geometric thinking and the development of different kinds of strategies so children benefit from the chance to play with both kinds.

Typically, once children move beyond trial and error with picture puzzles like the one shown here, they begin to attempt to align the shape of a puzzle piece with the shape of the hole or outline, as in Photo 4.4. This strategy is effective and emphasizes the recognition of shapes despite their rotation, and helps to develop the ability to hold a mental image of a geometric figure. Janelle, a 4-year-old who worked on this puzzle during free play, relied primarily on this strategy, attempting to find pieces that matched the outlined shapes on the back of the puzzle and turn them to fit. However, many of the pieces were extremely similar, which made this task difficult. The teacher's only interaction with Janelle, delivered as she passed by, was to compliment her on her hard

Figure 4.2. Highlighting Geometry in Block Play

Play Context	CCSD	Mathematical Ideas	Teacher Comments or Questions
Building towers with varyingly sized blocks	K.G.A.1 K.G.A.2 K.G.B.4 K.G.B.6 1.G.A.2	Naming shapes Comparing 3-D figures Composing figures	"What kinds of blocks did you use?" "How are those two blocks different?" "Do you think you could keep the tower going with the smaller blocks?"
Building from a model or diagram	K.G.A.2 K.G.B.4 K.G.B.5 1.G.A.2	Recognizing geometric figures in the real world Composing simple shapes or figures	"What kind of block do you need to make that?" "Which of these blocks does that look most like?" "How is your structure different from the picture?" "What does the part you can't see look like?" "Can you match up the faces like in the picture?"
Composing and decomposing composite shapes	K.G.B.4 K.G.B.5 1.G.A.2	Recognizing relationships between shapes and figures (e.g. triangles can make rectangles)	"What else might fit in that space?" "Is there a different way to build that?" "Can you make the same thing with more/fewer blocks?" "How many green blocks does it take to make a purple block?"
Building complicated structures or filling in an area	K.G.B.4 1.G.A.2 2.G.A.1	Using geometric language Recognizing and drawing shapes	"I wonder how many little blocks it will take to fill up that space." "Maybe you could take something apart to make it fit." "Do you think you could make the same tower on the other side?" "Can you tell me about what you made?" "Do you think you could draw a picture of what you did?"

Photo 4.4. Camden Completes a Picture Jigsaw Puzzle

work and urge her to keep at it. After about 10 minutes, Janelle grew frustrated and left the puzzle table.

Meanwhile, Danisha completed the same puzzle in about 6 minutes. Sometimes she relied on Janelle's strategy of shape recognition, particularly when placing the pieces with flat sides along the edge, but often she relied on imagining the picture as a whole, making comments like: "This piece got spots so it's the giraffe. That's over here." Danisha moved back and forth between considering the shapes of individual pieces and recognizing each piece as a smaller section of the larger image. This ability to decompose the big picture not only made her a more efficient puzzle solver, but also allowed her to develop the broader skill of composing and decomposing figures, which could be drawn on in other contexts. Over time in the classroom, the children who had developed multiple strategies for solving puzzles tended to spend more of their free time working on them, and thus became even more efficient at manipulating and visualizing shapes, while children who relied on trial and error tended to give up on puzzles before they gained the satisfaction of solving them. Rarely, if ever, did teachers in the classroom intervene to explicitly address puzzle-solving skills. However, by carefully scaffolding puzzles, by explicitly naming strategies used by other children, and by suggesting particular strategies in the right moment, teachers could help all children become more successful at solving puzzles.

Puzzle frames designed for pattern blocks provide a relatively easy way of providing geometric puzzles for children. These puzzles are easy to find and to construct with varying levels of difficulty so that all children can experience success and develop their abilities to recognize and manipulate shapes and to compose and decompose figures. Figure 4.3 was constructed with the "shape tool" on the National Council of Teachers of Mathematics Illuminations website (www.illuminations. nctm.org) where children can manipulate blocks on screen and teachers can print frames for use in their classroom.

Figure 4.3. Pattern Block Puzzle

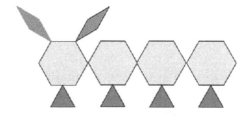

Many ready-made frames can also be found online and in teacher resource books. Figure 4.4 lists some online resources. The caterpillar frame is a relatively simple design, offering children color as a support in locating the correct shape and using relatively few blocks. Still, children must recognize the correct shapes and align them properly. As children become more skilled, black-and-white frames can be used as well as designs that require students to compose shapes using multiple blocks.

Teachers need to make conscious choices about what puzzles to make available at different times of the year, both to maintain interest and also to offer a continuous challenge to students who may be able to complete familiar puzzles with little thinking at all. New or challenging puzzles can be introduced before play times to generate interest and to highlight useful strategies. Figure 4.5 offers ideas for kinds of questions teachers might ask during puzzle play to support children's thinking.

EXPLORING POSSIBILITIES WITH DOLLS AND HOUSEKEEPING

Blocks and puzzles offer two clear play-based contexts for children to explore spatial relationships and to develop visual reasoning. However, the classroom is filled with other opportunities to experiment with geometric ideas. Children can cut out and describe shapes while working

Figure 4.4. Online Sites for Puzzle Play

NCTM's Illuminations: www.illuminations.nctm.org

> dynamic paper
>
> geometric solids
>
> patch tool
>
> shape cutter
>
> shape tool

National Library of Virtual Manipulatives: www.nlvm.usu.edu

> pattern blocks
>
> pentominoes
>
> tangrams
>
> tessellations
>
> triominoes

Figure 4.5. Highlighting Geometry in Puzzle Play

Play Context	CCSD	Mathematical Ideas	Teacher Comments or Questions
Picture Puzzles	K.G.A.2 K.G.B.6	Rotating shapes to match Composing and decomposing pictures Creating a mental image	"Where do you see the flat sides?" "What part of the picture do you think that is?" "Can you figure out which pieces go on the bottom of the puzzle and which go on top?" "Which colors go together?" "Can you see the finished puzzle in your mind?"
Geometric Puzzles	K.G.A.1 K.G.A.2 K.G.B.6 1.G.A.3	Naming shapes Recognizing shapes regardless of orientation Composing figures Creating and using composite shapes	"Can you solve that same puzzle another way?" "What's the most/least shapes you could use to make that?" "Which shapes can you see in the picture right now?" "What kinds of shapes do you know how to make with the pattern blocks?"

with play dough and construction paper, and in drawing they can both practice creating regular figures as well as varied 2-dimensional representations of the world. In fact, when studying the relationship between play and the ability to design block structures in formal tasks, researchers found that children who spent larger quantities of time on art-related tasks performed better than children who did not (Caldera et al., 1999). Play with housekeeping and with dolls has not been empirically studied in relation to developing geometric understandings; however, these sorts of toys can offer rich experiences for children and are important for teachers to keep in mind when thinking about locating mathematics in their classrooms, particularly for girls who may spend more of their choice time in these spaces.

At the most basic level, pretend play itself develops ways of thinking that support mathematical understandings broadly. As children engage in pretend play, they develop their abilities to represent one object as two things at once and to create mental representations (Lillard, 1993). For example, when a child pretends to feed her baby from a bowl of beads, she recognizes the objects as both beads and baby food, and as two playmates work together to create their "house" in the corner of the classroom, they may build mental representations of bedrooms, front porches, and laundry rooms that exist only in their minds. This sort of thinking is very similar to what older students will rely on to make sense of the idea that a line on a page is both the line on the page, but also an imaginary line that extends throughout infinite space.

More particularly, working with pretend food, dolls, and doll clothes offers opportunities for children to manipulate shapes in a variety of ways. For example, when Jamal cleaned up at the end of play time by folding a square blanket in half and then half again, he had the chance to develop an understanding of symmetry as well as how rectangles could be decomposed into other shapes. Similarly, when Alisha and her friends sat together and talked as they folded a basket of baby clothes, they had the chance to find lines of symmetry in a variety of shapes and to fold and refold until they got the match just right. Teachers could ask students questions in these moments ("Do you think you can fold all the clothes exactly in half? Why is that?"), or could simply say in passing, "You are matching those up just right" to draw the girls' attention to the mathematical work they were doing.

In the kitchen, placemat diagrams that show where to put the plate, fork, knife, and cup can teach not only table-setting but can also provide experiences for children to match 2-dimensional representations with 3-dimensional objects, and fruit and vegetables that can be "cut" and stuck back together allow children the chance to experiment with what happens when they break apart 3-D objects. Stocking the kitchen with materials that encourage students to make, cut, and serve foods like circular pizzas and square tarts can also provide opportunities to experiment with decomposing and composing shapes. These materials could be made out of play dough, cardboard, or purchased sets. Drawing pictures of their creations provides a chance for children to practice representing physical objects on a 2-D page. Suggesting tasks at the beginning of playtime might also give students a focus for their work, such as "I wonder how many different ways you could cut up a pizza," or "I would love to see a picture of your cake after you design it."

BRINGING BLOCKS, PUZZLES, AND DOLLS INTO FORMAL LESSONS

Of course if teachers are involved during playtime and mindful of the mathematics children explore independently, they can highlight a great deal of mathematics for the children. In addition, as discussed in Chapter 3, allowing children to make plans before playing and to share stories of their work afterward, provides additional opportunities for learning. However, children will need systematic, intentional instruction in geometry as well. This instruction can be most effective if it is linked with the play experiences children have during free time, both because it builds on understandings they have already developed, and because it can provide new ways of thinking that children can draw on to make their play more complex.

Although Chapter 10 will go into more depth about designing play-based formal lessons, the end of this chapter will provide a few suggestions for activities particularly related to geometry, including centers, tasks, and warm-ups and transition activities.

Centers

Centers can be productive in any classroom because they provide all children with the opportunity to engage with particular tasks, while minimizing the number of materials needed. In particular, classroom sets of wooden blocks can be very expensive and it can be overwhelming to think about finding the resources to buy enough for all the children in your class. However, a block-building center designed to serve four children requires far fewer materials. In addition, centers can provide a space to inject play and exploration into tightly scheduled days. First, 2nd- or 3rd-grade teachers—and in some districts even prekindergarten and kindergarten teachers—may find it hard to provide free play during the day. Centers provide a space where some play can happen. For classrooms where free play happens regularly, centers can provide a space for helping children mathematize their play, as well as to develop new skills that they can then practice during free time. Labeling center cards with the CCSS or with other district guidelines may help administrators and other visitors recognize the important mathematical work going on in centers.

One easy center to create involves taking pictures of wooden block or Lego creations (such as those shown in Photos 4.5 and 4.6) and asking children to recreate them.

Photo 4.5. Block Structure to Copy

Photo 4.6. Lego Block Structure to Copy

This activity encourages children to move between multiple representations of geometric figures, to manipulate images in their minds, and, if done with partners, to practice using geometric vocabulary to describe what they are doing. Teachers can take pictures of designs that they or other students create and choose particular pictures to develop new ways of playing with blocks in the classroom. After many experiences with activities like this, children could build block structures behind a file folder and then use only spoken language to help a partner recreate their structures.

Of course puzzles, both picture and geometric, can simply be offered as a center. However, center time also provides an opportunity for teachers to make conscious choices about scaffolding students' thinking. A series of pattern block puzzles could be arranged in order of difficulty and children could complete one before moving on to the next. If computers are available, students could also experiment with sites like the "shape tool" on the NCTM Illuminations website, which allows students to solve puzzles in a virtual environment and also to create pattern block puzzles for their friends to solve. More advanced activities could involve guidelines to follow in creating figures, including the number of shapes to be used or the ways in which certain figures must touch (i.e., a hexagon must share one edge with a triangle).

Play in the housekeeping area could be drawn on in centers where cutouts of paper doll clothes could be used to explore lines of symmetry. Students can cut out images of shirts, pants, dresses, and skirts and fold the "laundry" along lines of symmetry. Additionally students could create diagrams of "houses" they would like to create in either the housekeeping area or with blocks. Creating these maps supports the ability to create abstract representations and to think about figures as symbols

for objects in the real world. Finally, centers could provide a space for
children to engage in open play and exploration in classrooms where
such time is otherwise not available. If students do not ever get to play
on their own, teachers may want to create one or two centers where
children are allowed to build with wooden or Lego blocks or explore
puzzles without set tasks.

Tasks

During free play, teachers are likely to notice that children are not exploring the mathematics as deeply as possible. (Children, of course, have
other agendas during play.) Or, teachers may be working in environments where they feel unable to provide free play experiences for their
young students, but may still want to open up some opportunities for
exploration and bring the joy of play into their mathematics lessons.
Chapter 9 will go into depth on planning play-based lessons; however,
here are a few ideas for tasks that are closely connected to geometry.

Formal lessons provide opportunities for teachers to link mathematical vocabulary to shapes and figures students may be using during play,
and to support children in moving toward more complex ways of playing with materials they use routinely. Many of the same materials used
during free play support formal lessons, and the use of the same materials can help children make connections between the formal mathematics
lessons and play. For example, teachers might describe a block structure
or a pattern block puzzle using geometric language (hexagon, square-
rectangle, edge, corner, etc.) and have students create the figure on their
desks. Figure 4.6 presents important geometric vocabulary that could be
highlighted in play contexts. Pictures of finished figures can be shown
on an interactive white board and students can modify their creations to
match the image on the screen. Teachers can also talk students through
creating written representations of their figures. Students may need guidance in learning how to use isometric dot paper to represent 3-D objects
and can be encouraged to trace and label pattern block designs. Another
possibility is encouraging students to find multiple ways of creating the
same figure and recording which blocks or shapes are used. These activities support students' abilities to compose and decompose figures, skills
that are emphasized in the CCSS. Conversation during these activities
can also help children learn to recognize figures like triangles and rectangles, regardless of their orientation.

Figure 4.6. Key Vocabulary for Puzzle and Block Play

above	circle	edge
below	square-rectangle*	corner
beside	triangle	face
in front of	rectangle	
next to	side	

*Young children often develop the incorrect idea that a square is not a rectangle. Using this language can help them recognize a square as a "special" rectangle (NRC, 2009).

Research has also shown that using stories with students to prompt their block-building and puzzle-solving can support the creation of complex structures, which require more advanced geometric thinking (Casey, Erkut, Cedar, & Young, 2008; Casey, Kersh, & Young, 2004). Stories that encourage students to experiment with creating figures with pattern blocks or tangrams or that encourage students to build more complicated structures with blocks, such as those with arches, enclosures, or symmetry, can be motivational for many students and provide ideas for others. Figure 4.7 features books that might inspire children's geometric thinking. After teachers introduce these books in formal lessons, they can be freely available during play time or in centers.

Warm-Ups and Transitions

There are many quick activities related to geometry that teachers can do at the start of a lesson or during a transition that will help students think of their play in more mathematical contexts. When teachers introduce

Figure 4.7. Books to Inspire Geometry Play

Grandfather Tang's Story by Ann Tompert

The Greedy Triangle by Marilyn Burns

The Shape of Things by Dayle Ann Dodds

Block Building for Children by Lester Walker

Changes, Changes by Pat Hutchins

Block City by Robert Louis Stevenson

Building Structures with Young Children by Ingrid Chalufour and Karen Worth mathematical concepts in stories or in other contexts, children are more likely to take up these ideas during play (Wager, 2014). Many activities can be done with an interactive white board or overhead projector. Pictures of pattern block puzzles, block structures, and tangrams, which can all be easily found on the Internet by searching for images, can be flashed on the screen for several seconds. Students can then be asked to describe what they saw. This provides opportunities to practice naming figures, points of contact like edges or faces, and decomposing figures (K.G.B.4; 1.G.A.1; 1.G.A.2; 2.G.A.1). The images may also give ideas to children of things they can build during their free time.

Another activity involves taking a single wooden block or pattern block and hiding it. The teacher then describes the features of the object and children guess what the object is. After practice, children can choose a figure and offer clues. A variation on this activity involves placing a figure in a bag, and asking children to identify it by touch. This activity forces children to focus on the features of a shape rather than visual identifiers—like the color of a pattern block. Teachers can also scatter pattern blocks across a projector screen and ask students to identify them. This can be helpful in demonstrating for children that orientation does not matter in naming a shape. Finally, another option for transition times is showing pictures of puzzles and block structures students in the class have created. If the class does not have a regular time for sharing, this sort of activity can motivate children to both create new structures and can provide ideas for other students' future creations. Although the activities mentioned here are not play, they do offer teachers a chance to attach mathematical vocabulary to materials used during play and provide a way of motivating students to expand their play in the future.

Typically in formal geometry lessons in the early grades, children do learn to identify shapes and describe their features. However, they often do not have the opportunities to develop the broader visualization skills, such as creating and manipulating a mental image, that are vital for more advanced work in geometry. Play offers an important context where children can develop the visual ways of thinking and geometric problem-solving strategies that will support their mathematics learning much later in their school years.

CHAPTER 5

Games and Action Figures
The Number and Operations Standards

After nearly 4 months of practicing counting to 20 orally and counting small sets individually, Mrs. Connor has decided that it's time to deepen her preschoolers' number sense. She draws four dots on her white board and asks Eliot to count them as she points.

Eliot: One, two, three, four.

Mrs. Connor: How many did you count?

Eliot: Four.

Mrs. Connor (writing a "4" above the dots): Suppose I put one more with it *[see Figure 5.1].* What do I need to say? Four plus how many?

Eliot: One.

Mrs. Connor: And how many in all?

Jaylen: Two!

Mrs. Connor: Count them *[pointing].*

Eliot: One, two, three, four, five.

Mrs. Connor (writing "+ 1 = 5" after the 4): Eliot can you read this?

Eliot: Four equals?

Mrs. Connor: Four *[pointing to the 4]* plus . . .

Eliot: Four plus one . . . equals *[looking at Mrs. Connor pointing]* five.

Mrs. Connor: Good job. Way to go.

Figure 5.1. Adding 4 + 1

Figure 5.2. Adding 3 + 1

$$3 \qquad + \qquad 1 \qquad = 4$$

After working with Eliot, Mrs. Connor then repeats the activity with a few other students. The next problem she presents on the white board looks like Figure 5.2. Although the child Mrs. Connor calls on reads this problem correctly, with the help of her pointing, many children on the back of the carpet whisper: "It's eight!" "That's eight!"

Scenes like the one above are common in preschool and kindergarten classrooms where teachers are unsure of what children need to know about number other than counting and the operations of addition and subtraction. This is particularly true in early childhood classrooms that do not have a formal mathematics curriculum to scaffold teachers' thinking. However, the leap from early counting to formal addition with symbols is significant, as demonstrated by the children's confusion in the episode above. Although Eliot is able to produce the correct answer, he does so primarily by counting and repeating after his teacher. When Jaylen calls out "two" and the children on the back of the carpet whisper "It's eight," they also show that they are still thinking about the problems as counting problems with little understanding of what the operation of addition means, what the symbols represent, or what words like "plus" or "equals" are supposed to convey. Their only experience with counting has been identifying the number of objects in a set. In order to productively engage with the operations of addition and subtraction, the children need first to develop a richer conception of number, where they can not only identify the quantities of sets, but where they can also understand numbers in relationship to each other, such as by identifying which is bigger, which is smaller, and what happens when sets are combined or broken apart.

Ideally, children in the early years will develop broad and deep understandings of number and number relationships before they are ever introduced to the formal vocabulary and symbols of addition and subtraction. Fortunately, play contexts in the early grades provide multiple meaningful opportunities for children to build these understandings; however, in order for this to happen teachers must themselves have a conception of early number work that extends beyond rote and meaningful counting.

BIG IDEAS IN EARLY NUMBER

The first skills young children must master in relation to number are counting orally, recognizing written number symbols, cardinality, and one-to-one correspondence (National Research Council, 2009). Nearly all children through experiences at home and in early schooling learn to recite the number list to 20 and to recognize written numbers. In addition, many activities in school that are regularly a part of preschool and kindergarten classrooms provide opportunities to practice these skills, such as activities around the calendar, singing counting songs, and reading math-related books. Teachers are very likely to prompt students to count orally and to read numbers when opportunities emerge. However, the development of cardinality and one-to-one correspondence generally receive less attention.

Cardinality is the ability to recognize that when one counts a set, the last number said names the quantity of the set. The classic test of cardinality involves asking a child to count the items in a set, listening for an answer, and then asking again how many items there are. Figure 5.3 provides an example of an assessment interview for two children, one of whom has developed cardinality and one who has not. Children who have cardinality generally will repeat their answer, while children who are still developing this skill will go back and recount. Children cannot develop cardinality solely through direct instruction. That is, they cannot simply be told that the last item in the count is the amount of the set. They must develop this knowledge for themselves through repeated recountings. Similarly, one-to-one correspondence also develops through repeated practice. Developing this concept means that children know that each number word must be matched with one and only one object in a set to be counted. Children who have one-to-one correspondence will not skip or double-count objects when counting, although children may master one-to-one correspondence with small sets of objects before being able to extend the skill to larger sets.

In thinking about early math instruction, it is important to recognize that whole-class activities provide few opportunities for children to develop cardinality and one-to-one correspondence (although they can be

Figure 5.3. The Cardinality Principle

Sadie Counting

Interviewer (placing 5 blocks in a line in front of Sadie): Can you count those for
    me?
Sadie (touching each block): 1, 2, 3, 4, 5
Interviewer: So how many are there all together?
Sadie (pushing the blocks into a pile and touching each one): 1, 2, 3, 4, 5
Interviewer: So how many is that?
Sadie (touching each block): 1, 2, 3, 4, 5

Claire Counting

Interviewer (placing 5 blocks in a line in front of Claire): Can you count those for
    me?
Claire (looking at each block as she counts): 1, 2, 3, 4, 5
Interviewer: How many are there all together?
Claire: 5. I said that.

---

very helpful for helping children to count orally and to recognize written numbers). To become fluent counters of objects, children must have
repeated practice counting objects that they can touch, making play and
small group settings ideal for developing these skills.

After these early counting skills develop, there are still a variety of
number relationships that children would benefit from developing before they begin to think about formal addition and subtraction. When
children can count fluently objects they can touch, they will benefit from
activities that would allow them to practice counting objects that are
hidden from view, which requires that they visualize the objects. For
example, students could count objects as they drop them into a cup, or
look at a collection of objects before a friend hides them and then count
how many there were. In addition, children can be supported in their
ability to "count on," or to start counting from a number other than
one, with or without objects (Steffe & Cobb, 1998). For example, a
child might have a family of three bears and then count bears that some-
one adds. A child who is counting on starts with the number "3" for the
original bear family, rather than counting over each time. Counting on is
useful for children when they begin to work on addition problems, but

they can master the skill within counting contexts before beginning to work on formal addition problems.

Finally, in the early grades children should develop a strong understanding of number relationships, which will support their work in mathematics throughout the elementary years. Children need experiences with activities and games that allow them to recognize sets of objects as more, less, and the same; to identify numbers as being one more or one less than a target number; to understand numbers in relation to the benchmarks of 5 and 10; and to compose and decompose numbers from 1–20, which means recognizing that the numbers can be broken apart and put together in various ways. For example, the number 4 could be thought of as 1 and 3; 2 and 2; and 3 and 1. It should be apparent that fluency with decomposing and composing will support work in addition and subtraction in later grades (Van de Walle, Karp, Bay-Williams, & Wray, 2007).

COUNTING AND COMPARISON
WITH ACTION FIGURES AND OTHER TOYS

Providing attractive collections of objects as toys in the preschool classroom offers children natural opportunities to count and compare. Children may make trains of cars and count to see who has the most, or make groups of animals and check to see that each group has the same number, as the little girl with the dinosaurs is doing in Photo 5.1.

Teachers can support these counting efforts by encouraging children to do more than simply count sets. Asking questions such as "Which pile has more animals?" or "How many more does Jenna have?" directs children toward more complex mathematics than simply asking "How many?" questions. In addition, when teachers see children counting toys, they can offer strategies to promote more successful counts, such as by asking children to touch each object as they count, or by offering possibilities for organizing the objects being counted. These informal counting moments also provide opportunities for teachers to observe children to assess their progress in terms of oral counting, one-to-one correspondence, and cardinality. Some children may perform more competently in these informal environments than in assessment contexts. Teachers can also elicit opportunities for children to practice counting skills by designing centers such as those described in Figure 5.4.

Photo 5.1. Chloe Counts Out Rows of 3 Dinosaurs

As children move into kindergarten and 1st grade, they need opportunities to make sense of larger sets of numbers. Collection toys can still be important for promoting these skills. Counting large sets of objects not only gives children opportunities to practice the counting sequence to 100, but also allows children to explore grouping objects for counting

Figure 5.4. Centers for Developing Early Number

1. Clothes Pin Number Line

Provide a basket of number cards for children. Fasten a 0 and 5 or 0 and 10 onto the clothesline. Ask children to pin numbers in the correct place. (This activity can be made more challenging by using larger numbers or by leaving some numbers out.)

2. Number Museum

Leave out small baskets and number cards. Children can fill baskets with the appropriate number of objects for their cards and line them up on a bookshelf in order to make a number museum. (Children can then take the cards out and invite their friends to place the cards in the correct basket.)

3. More/Less/Same

Create multiple sets of three dishes, with one in each set labeled "more," "less," and "the same." Provide containers of different objects, such as bears, cars, keys, or shells. Children can play on their own or in pairs by flipping a number card over and creating sets of more, less, and the same for each number.

4. Composing and Decomposing Numbers

Provide children with mats, number cards 1–5 or 1–10 depending on the grade level, and a set of different colored objects such as bears, cars, fruits, or any other available manipulatives. Invite children to find as many ways as they can to make each number. (For example: two blue bears and three red bears; four yellow bears and one red bear; etc.) If you have a set of stamps or pictures that can be cut out and glued that match your objects, children can create representations of their work for a poster in the room.

in various ways. Teachers can suggest making groupings of "easy" numbers like 5 and 10 as a way of helping children get comfortable with benchmark numbers and develop a sense of place value. Large collections can also be used to invite children to engage in art projects that encourage counting, such as by making posters for "25," "50," or "100." By providing engaging materials, such as pompoms, buttons, colored pasta, and sequins, teachers can invite children to engage in these projects as part of choice time. The counting of physical objects is important throughout the early grades in order to help children develop cardinality, one-to-one correspondence, and number relationships. In the primary grades, counting activities often take place in the context of the calendar.

However, generally when counting days of the week or popsicle sticks, only one child (or sometimes just the teacher) has the opportunity to touch the objects being counted. Simply watching others count is unlikely to do much to help children develop early number sense.

SUPPORTING GAME-BASED PLAY

In kindergarten, 1st, and 2nd grades, games can provide important opportunities for children to develop more complex number relationships. When rolling the dice, they can think about how many more or less their roll was than their friends'; they can figure out how many more spaces they need to go on the board and whether their roll was enough; and in carefully designed or chosen games, they can be invited to make decisions about how to divide a number rolled among multiple pawns. Of course, games can be used in prekindergarten as well; however, navigating the social and emotional experience of game play is often challenging for young children, and can make focusing on the mathematics difficult. Even in the early elementary years, teachers may want to introduce simple games like *Candyland* before providing access to more complex games. Before they can engage productively with mathematics during game play, children need to have multiple experiences managing the feelings involved in winning and losing (including the tension many children experience during game play when they do not know if they will win or lose), as well as negotiating the social practices involved in games, such as turn-taking and distributing materials. However, once these skills are mastered games can provide a highly motivating context for children to develop number relationships around more and less, anchors of 5 and 10, and composing and decomposing numbers.

Researchers have found that playing linear board games can improve children's competencies related to counting, estimating, and comparing numbers (Siegler & Ramani, 2009). Positive changes in performance have been documented even with relatively brief engagements with games. For example, Ramani and Siegler (2008) found that playing a linear board game with students for four 15-minute sessions improved children's performance on number line tasks. Incidentally, they found that playing games that had circular trails to move around did not have the same effect (Siegler & Ramani, 2009). In another study, the same pair of researchers found that playing linear games had more positive impacts on children's abilities to estimate, compare, and identify numbers than other kinds of activities related to number, and that these gains were even more significant for low-income children (Ramani & Siegler, 2011). Researchers in other contexts have demonstrated similar findings (e.g., Wang & Hung, 2010; White & Bull, 2008).

Commercially Available Games

Any games that require counting and movement along a series of spaces can be productive for young children. Children must count the correct number of spaces. In dice games, they have opportunities to recognize number patterns. And as they think about winning, they pose problems for themselves, such as: How far ahead of me is she? What do I need to win? How many more spaces until the end of the board? Figure 5.5 provides suggestions for scaffolding children's numeric thinking during game play.

In introducing games to primary classrooms, it makes sense to introduce one at a time so children have opportunities to master the game play and to thoughtfully choose games so that the majority of the intellectual challenges are around mathematics, rather than the process of the game. It can also be useful to think about how long games take to play, both in terms of children's attention levels and in terms of the time you have available for free play. Thinking about games in terms of both their mathematical and social complexity can provide teachers with a way of determining which games are appropriate for their children and which games should be introduced first. Here are a few games that successfully incorporate different mathematical skills related to number, organized for less to more mathematically and socially complex. Figure 5.6 shows relationships between games and the Common Core State Standards.

Figure 5.5. Scaffolding Game Play

Often adult prompts can focus children's attention on mathematics during game play. Here are some ideas for questions to ask while observing:

- How many more do you need to win?
- Who has the most?
- Can you touch the spaces while you count?
- If you get a 2, what will happen?
- How far ahead of you is she?

Figure 5.6. Common Core State Standards and Math Games

Grade Level	Standard	Games
Kindergarten	K.CC.A.1. Count to 100 by 1s and 10s.	*Count Your Chickens* *HiHo! Cherry-O* *Chutes and Ladders* Teacher-designed linear board games (use designed spinners or dice move by 10s or 1s)
	K.CC.A.2. Count forward beginning from a given number with the known set.	Teacher designed linear board games: Encourage children to count forward by saying the number of the space their pawn is on and then counting each square (for example, if a child rolls a 3, and is on the 5 square, she should say "6, 7, 8," not "1, 2, 3."
	K.CC.B.4. Understand the relationship between numbers and quantities; connect counting to cardinality.	*Count Your Chickens* *HiHo! Cherry-O*
	K.CC.B.5. Count to answer "how many?" questions	*Count Your Chickens* Cooperative grabbing game: Provide a jar of small items (e.g., buttons, cotton balls, blocks). Two children each take one handful, count how many they have all together, and record the answer. They then return the materials and keep playing until they cannot beat their previous total as a pair.
	K.CC.C.7. Compare two numbers between 1 and 10 presented as written numerals.	"War"-style card games with decks of cards that contain multiple copies of each numeral 1–10.
	K.OA.A.4. For any number from 1 to 9, find the number that makes 10 when added to the given number.	Make ten Card Games: Play games modeled on "Go Fish" or "Concentration" with decks of cards with the numerals 1–9. Children create pairs or matches that equal 10.
	K.OA.A.3. Decompose numbers less than or equal to 10 into pairs in more than one way.	*Sorry!* Make "X" Card Games: Play as with "Make 10" only choose different focal numbers so children can find ways to make 5, 6, 7, 8, or 9.

	Standard	Activities
Grade 1	1.NBT.A.1. Count to 120 starting at any number less than 120.	*Sorry!* *Trouble* Teacher-designed linear board games. Children can decorate boards. Play can be changed by using different kinds of dice (large numbers, small numbers, numerals, dots, etc.).
	1.NBT.C.6. Subtract multiples of 10 in the range of 10–90 from multiples of 10 in the range 10–90.	Teacher-designed linear board games where the goal is to get from 90 to 0. Children can move by turning over playing cards numbered in multiples of 10.
	1.NBT.B.3. Compare two 2-digit numbers based on meanings of the tens and ones digits.	"War"-style card games with decks of cards that include numbers to 99.
Grade 2	2.OA.B.2. Fluently add and subtract within 20 using mental strategies.	Face Up Concentration: Lay out 25 cards with numerals 0–19 face up between two players. Players must choose two cards and then correctly add them mentally to keep them. Players can check each other's answers with calculators.
	2.OA.C.4. Use addition to find the total number of objects arranged in rectangular arrays with up to 5 rows and up to 5 columns.	Concentration: Make decks with sets of matching numerals and arrays up to 5 by 5. Players turn over cards and try to create matches between the arrays and the numerals.
	2.NBT.A.2. Count within 1,000; skip-count by 5s, 10s, and 100s.	Teacher-designed linear board games that have spaces labeled to 1,000. Students can move using playing cards or spinners that have 5s, 10s, and 100s.
	2.NBT.A.4. Compare two 3-digit numbers based on meanings of the 100s, 10s, and 1s digits.	"War"-style card games with decks of cards that include numbers to 999.

Count Your Chickens *by Peaceable Kingdom Press.* This game makes a nice introduction to game play because it is a cooperative game, which means all of the children playing together win or lose as a group. As a result, children still must learn to take turns, but they do not have anxiety around winning and losing. The game, which has a picture-based spinner, requires that children move their marker to a space on the board indicated by the picture on the spinner. Children must then count the number of spaces they moved and then count that many "chicken" pieces, providing two opportunities to count with one-to-one correspondence. The game is over when all the players reach the end of the board. The players win if all of the chickens have been collected at this time. If not, they lose to the fox.

HiHo! Cherry-O *by Hasbro.* In this game, children spin to see how many cherries they should take off their cherry tree, which holds ten cherries. The spinner shows pictures of cherries, so students do not need to be able to recognize written numerals in order to play. The largest number of cherries that students take off during any spin is three, making the game productive for children who are just mastering one-to-one correspondence and for children who are just learning to take turns and to lose gracefully. The game moves relatively quickly, making the frustration factor low, and can be played with little adult guidance after children are taught what the symbols on the spinner mean. In addition to counting, the format of the game also encourages students to figure out how many more they need to win, whether they have more or less than their friends, and with support, combinations of numbers that make 10. This game provides opportunities for young children to practice meaningful counting in a game context that isn't too confusing or frustrating, unlike the game described in Figure 5.7.

Dominoes. The most common of these tiles have two sets of dot patterns on each block representing the numbers 0 to 6 and can be used flexibly to emphasize different mathematical skills. At the most basic level, children can draw seven to ten blocks each and choose a starter block for the middle of the board. Players add blocks one at a time by matching a dot pattern on one of their dominoes with one showing on the table. If the player has no block to play, another block can be chosen from the leftover pile. The game is over when one player gets rid of all of his or her dominoes. This version of the game allows children to practice

Figure 5.7. What About *Chutes and Ladders*?

Chutes and Ladders is a game commonly identified as a counting game for young children; however, this game can often be frustrating for young children. The goal of the game is to reach the end of a 100-space board, sometimes taking short cuts up ladders and sometimes going backward down chutes. The numbers are arranged in rows on the board, with every other row going up from right to left instead of left to right. This arrangement can make counting confusing for young children. The mathematics of the game is primarily counting up by a number from 1 to 6, which would be most appropriate for preschool and kindergarten children. However, the length of the game, the magnitude of the numbers of the board, and the confusing layout of the numbers make the game difficult for these children to access. Older children who might benefit from problems like adding 6 to 35 are unlikely to find the game particularly engaging or attractive, and there is little in the game itself that would encourage older kids to move using mental arithmetic rather than simply counting spaces. That said, if you have *Chutes and Ladders* and your children enjoy it, go ahead and use it. However, if you are building a game collection, you may find it productive to start with other choices.

---

recognizing visual representations of small numbers as well as counting in order to confirm their recognitions. The game can be modified so that instead of matching identical numbers, players must align patterns that are 1 more or 1 less or equal to 5. Many other versions of the game can be found online.

Trouble *by Hasbro*. This game, where players move four pawns around the board using dice rolls, offers children opportunities to recognize written numerals on the dice as well as to count. During each turn, players must decide which pawn to move and then count the appropriate number of spaces. Because of the multiple pawns, this means that players might decide to count out moves for multiple pieces before deciding on a course of action. As a result, the game encourages players to count quickly and to move toward counting without touching each space on the board. In addition, players can send their opponents' pieces back to the beginning by landing on them, offering the opportunity to make counting estimates about when this kind of move might be a possibility. Of course, this feature of the game can also be frustrating to young children, who might need adult guidance as they get used to this aspect of the game.

Sorry by Hasbro. As with *Trouble*, players in *Sorry* must move four pawns around the board from start to home. However, *Sorry* offers more complex game play as well as slightly more complex mathematics than *Trouble*. Rather than using a dice, players draw cards to move. The largest card is a 12 and the 7 card can be split between two pawns, allowing children to practice breaking 7 apart in various ways as they think through strategies. In addition, a variety of features of the board, such as "slide spaces" and "safety spaces," encourage students to think about strategy and how to use their card most wisely.

A variety of other games can provide support for children's early number skills. The challenge when evaluating commercial games is to consider the amount of time students will spend understanding and negotiating the rules of the game versus the amount of time students will spend engaging in mathematics. In addition, it is important to consider whether the mathematics is at an appropriate level for the children in your classroom. This is most difficult for primary grades classrooms where children have already mastered number recognition and meaningful counting. Finding commercial games that engage children in mathematics related to comparing numbers, adding and subtracting, counting to 100, and anchors of 5 and 10 can be challenging. This is when drawing on games developed in early childhood mathematics curricula may be helpful.

Educational Games

Many curricula for young children include games explicitly designed to teach mathematics. One big benefit of these games is that the mathematics highlighted is likely to be appropriate to the children in the grade level, although sometimes the games themselves can be less attractive to children, either because of the design of the materials or the structure of the game. One way to make materials more engaging to children is to invite them to decorate or design materials, such as by drawing game boards, decorating the backs of playing cards, or creating pawns from clay or other materials. Offering a variety of games at appropriate levels of mathematical challenge for the children in the room is important to sustaining interest in game play. Many games suggested in mathematics curricula are based on either card games or board games. Teachers can of course design their own games (or find examples online) using these structures. In deciding which games to introduce, it is important to think about the kinds of mathematics being highlighted by the game and the needs of particular children. Below is a description of some of the mathematical ideas that can be highlighted through various board and card games.

Card Games. One way to vary the challenge of a mathematical card game is by intentionally designing the kinds of cards used. Games may be played with cards that have numerals, number words, dot patterns, pictures, or some combination of these. Children with different needs can play the same game with different cards so that children who need help recognizing numerals play with one deck, while children who need help practicing one-to-one correspondence play with another deck. Although the details of games vary across curricula, most games are based on a few of key forms of game play:

1. *Matching Games.* In these games, children match cards that go together, either by trying to remember where pairs of cards are in a layout on a table or by trying to create pairs of cards with rules similar to *Go Fish*. These games can be useful to children who are learning to match quantities, numerals, and number words. Alternatively, matches could be two cards that equal a target number like 10 as a way of supporting composing and decomposing of numbers.
2. *Set Games.* In these games, children typically start with five to seven cards in their hands and put down "sets" when they can, similar to the games like *Rummy*. The goal is to get rid of all of one's cards. What constitutes a set can vary based on the identified mathematical skills. For example, children could put down any set of cards that equal 5, 10, or 20.
3. *Comparison Games.* In these games, a deck of cards is divided between two players who stack their cards face down in front of them. Players turn cards over at the same time and the person whose card is greater wins, as in the classic game *War*. Variations of the game can be introduced so that the winning card must be exactly 1 or 2 more than the other card. In addition, the difficulty of the game can be controlled by playing with decks that go to 10, 20, or 100.

Board Games. As discussed in the previous section, there are a variety of commercial games that use paths on a board to structure play. The advantage of curriculum- or teacher-designed games is that the board can be designed to highlight mathematical thinking. Research (Siegler & Ramani, 2008, 2009; Siegler, 2009) has demonstrated that playing linear board games—even for as short a time as four 15-minute sessions— can significantly improve children's abilities to estimate magnitudes in a linear way. In other words, linear board games help children recognize that 5 is the same distance from 3 as it is from 7. In their work, researchers Ramani and Siegler have found that game boards that mimic number lines are particularly helpful for young children. In other words, using boards with equal-sized, numbered squares that extend in a straight, rather than a circular or curving pattern is most helpful. In addition, they have demonstrated that children learn counting, comparison, and arithmetic more efficiently from playing well-designed games than they do from standard early number activities, like saying the number sequence or counting objects (Siegler & Ramani, 2009). For the youngest children, games that ask them to move across boards numbered from 1 to 10 or from 1 to 20 are probably most helpful. Because even relatively short bursts of play have been shown to have impact, games can be quite simple and still be adequately engaging. The idea of these games could be extended for older children by using two dice to roll and a board that goes to 100. In addition, numbered dice that go as high as 20 could be used. These sorts of games are likely to encourage children to develop strategies for mentally adding numbers, rather than counting out each square if the roll is quite large. Children may have to play the game repeatedly before they come to trust their own and the partner's strategies in favor of counting each space. However, this process of verification could be a valuable opportunity for learning.

Game-Based Lessons

Although teachers can support students in choosing to play games independently during choice times, independent game play can be supported by adult introductions to the rules and to the mathematics of the games. Children are more likely to negotiate game play successfully if they agree on the procedures for game play, and they are more likely to play in ways that highlight mathematics if adults help them to develop routines for play. Small groups make excellent structures for introducing gaming routines to young children. Introducing games in large groups makes it difficult for all children to see the materials, and some children give up trying and become disengaged. In small groups, all children can quickly get their hands on materials. In addition, games introduced in small groups can be chosen or modified for their mathematical appropriateness. Young students who are still working on counting and cardinality to 20 may benefit from playing *Count Your Chickens* or *HiHo! Cherry-O*; however, students who have mastered these skills may be more challenged by games that require counting to higher numbers or comparing numbers. There may be some cases where teachers want to have their entire classes playing the same games, such as when a 2nd-grade class is learning to compare numbers; however, for the most part, games are easy ways to differentiate instruction. Even when playing with the same game structure, teachers can modify games by varying the numbers children work with on dice, spinners, or cards.

In designing a game-based small-group lesson, teachers can think about both the mathematics they want to highlight as well as the social challenges that children might experience when playing games, and help children to develop strategies for dealing with these. After establishing that children feel comfortable playing games, teachers can also show children where the games are stored and encourage students to play games during free choice time. Games should be rotated frequently, to keep up with children's mathematical learning, but also to encourage interest.

Finally, in thinking about game-based lessons, teachers may want to think about having debriefings with children after playing either in small- or whole-group settings. One reason to hold a debriefing in a whole-group setting, even if all children did not play the game, might be to generate interest about a game or to model a particularly useful strategy for other children in the class. For example, after game play, teachers might ask a child who played *Count Your Chickens* to model how he lined up his chicken pieces before counting them in order to highlight organizing in rows as a counting strategy. Similarly, a teacher could show sets of two number cards from a *War* card game and ask students to discuss how they decided which number was greater. These kinds of conversations can help children make links between the mathematics they engage with during game play and the mathematics they participate in during formal lessons.

CHAPTER 6

Which Is Longer?
What Holds More?
The Measurement Standards

When primary grade teachers introduce measurement tools and concepts, they tend to anticipate a host of problems: Students will not know how to align the ruler properly; students will confuse units of measurement; students will be unable to estimate volumes of containers appropriately. At the same time, many teachers feel pressured to introduce formal measurement tools quickly and to limit the time and messiness spent in exploring concepts like volume. For example, I have been in many classrooms in the early grades, where, during lessons on capacity only the teacher handled the demonstration containers of water, while children were expected to learn by watching passively. By attending to measurement concepts in play and designing spaces likely to solicit thinking about measurement, teachers in the earliest grades can play an important role in providing children with the foundational experiences they will need in order to productively engage with more formal measurement concepts later.

BIG IDEAS IN MEASUREMENT

Learning to recognize and talk about measurable attributes, or the quality of an object that can be measured, is the first big challenge for young children in measurement. Although it may seem obvious to adults, children must learn that when thinking about measuring an object, one can ask, among other attributes, about its length, its weight, or the quantity it can hold. In other words, children must come to recognize that an attribute like length can be applied to an almost infinite number of objects in the world: people, rooms, toys, doors, pets, and so on. In addition, they also must come to recognize which qualities of any given object matter when trying to figure out length. For example, children must understand that knowing which of two books is heavier does not allow one to make any judgments about length. This distinction can be tricky for young children because they have tended to think about comparisons in more general terms, such as by identifying which book is "bigger." Coming to understand that one attribute of any given object can be bigger, while another attribute of the same object can be smaller than the thing it's being compared to is significant intellectual work, and too often, too little attention is paid to helping children develop these ways of thinking. In fact, measurement is a surprisingly difficult strand of mathematics for U.S. students, with students historically performing less well on assessments of this strand than on assessments of number or geometry (Clements, 2003; Stephan & Clements, 2003; Thompson & Preston, 2004).

In moving children toward more sophisticated ideas of measurement, three kinds of activities are important: comparing, modeling measurement units (covering a distance to be measured with identical units), and using measurement tools (Van de Walle, Karp, Bay-Williams, & Wray, 2007). The goal of comparing activities is to help children learn to recognize and name measurable attributes, while activities that involve modeling with measurable units are designed to help children see that any unit of the same size can be used to measure an attribute. Both of these kinds of activities are important to help children understand how to appropriately use formal measurement tools later. For example, if children have many experiences measuring length with links, teddy bears, or other small objects, they are more likely to recognize that it is the space between lines on a ruler that must be counted, rather than the lines or the numbers themselves, reducing the likelihood that children will misread the ruler by either ignoring the space on the ruler before the hash marks begin or by counting the lines instead of spaces to produce their answers. Figure 6.1 shows how the CCSSM measurement standards for K–2 can be thought about across these three kinds of activities.

As demonstrated in Figure 6.1, activities in prekindergarten and kindergarten should focus on the comparing of attributes and the development of a vocabulary specific to each attribute (i.e., "longer" or "heavier" rather than "bigger"). In 1st grade, the emphasis is on using

Figure 6.1. CCSSM Measurement Standards K–2

	Comparing	Modeling Measurement Units	Using Measurement Tools
Kindergarten	Describe measurable attributes of objects, such as length or weight. Describe several measurable attributes of a single object. Directly compare two objects with a measurable attribute in common, to see which object has "more of"/"less of" the attribute, and describe the difference.		
Grade 1	Order three objects by length.	Compare the lengths of two objects indirectly by using a third object. Express the length of an object as a whole number of length units, by laying multiple copies of a shorter object end to end; understand that the length measurement of an object is the number of same-size length units that span it with no gaps or overlaps.	

Grade 2

Measure the length of an object by selecting and using appropriate tools such as rulers, yardsticks, meter sticks, and measuring tapes.

Measure the length of an object twice, using length units of different lengths for the two measurements; describe how the two measurements relate to the size of the unit chosen.

Estimate lengths using units of inches, feet, centimeters, and meters.

Measure to determine how much longer one object is than another, expressing the length difference in terms of a standard length unit.

nonstandard tools to measure, such as paper clips, and on comparing objects to focal objects to make comparisons. For example, students might be given a length of string and asked to find materials in the classroom that are longer, shorter, or the same size. When engaging in these activities, it is important to continually direct children's attention to the units they are using and the ways in which they are using the units (Stephan & Clements, 2003). Students need help recognizing that when they measure, they are counting units of space (as marked by the objects they are using to measure), that they must use units that are of equal size, and that they cannot leave spaces between units or overlap units if they want their measure to be accurate.

It is not until 2nd grade that formal measurement tools are addressed in the CCSSM. Although there is probably little to be gained by introducing prekindergarten and kindergarten students to formal measurement tools, beyond allowing them to think about which attributes they are most useful for measuring, young children may be ready, in informal contexts, to do some kinds of modeling with units to help prepare them for more formal work later. In addition, although the 1st- and 2nd-grade measurement standards are primarily focused on length, investigations of capacity and weight by young children can be useful, both in helping them to recognize that measurement can be used for a variety of attributes and for developing a set of concrete experiences that can be activated in later grades, when the study of weight and volume become a more prominent part of the curriculum.

TOYS THAT ENCOURAGE COMPARISON

Early childhood classrooms that include regular time for play can provide important sites for children to build big conceptual ideas about measurement. This is particularly important because lessons in the upper grades often focus on the proper procedures for using measurement tools. There are many common toys and play contexts that provide incentive for children to engage in comparisons; however, teachers can be more intentional about highlighting particular toys, connecting measurement ideas across play contexts, and by engaging with students during play in ways that direct their attention to particular attributes and help them to use appropriate vocabulary.

Linking Toys

Toys that can be linked together to create long chains or towers naturally encourage children to experiment with making long structures and to engage in comparisons with the structures made by other children. Examples of toys that promote this kind of play include chain links (such as in Photo 6.1), snapping cubes, and Lego blocks.

In addition to making these toys available to children, teachers can engage students in thinking about measurement by encouraging them to make comparisons. In addition to seeing whose tower or chain is the longest, children can also use their towers to measure other objects in the classroom. Questions like: "Is your chain longer than the table?" can encourage children to begin these explorations as part of their play.

Photo 6.1. Mila Builds a Link Chain

Providing a site for record keeping is another way of both promoting interest in measurement toys and in prompting more complex thinking about measurement. Children could mark on butcher paper or sentence strips the heights of their towers or the lengths of their chains. If these paper records were posted on the walls of the classroom, other children could try to break records by creating a longer chain or tower. This kind of experimentation not only helps children learn to see, measure, and talk about the attribute of length, but also provides them with opportunities to think about how much longer one tower is than another. When children are ready, these kinds of questions can be explored with help from adults in the classroom.

Sensory Tables

The sensory tables common in many preschool and kindergarten classrooms provide ideal sights for children's investigations of capacity. Filling tables with pasta, rice, water, Styrofoam peanuts, or any other pourable substance makes it possible for children to fill and empty containers. Simply having the experience of filling and emptying many different-sized containers provides children with some background for understanding the attribute of capacity, particularly if in conversations about the table, adults are careful to talk with children about which containers can "hold more" rather than about which are "bigger." This kind of language helps to differentiate the attribute of capacity from that of length. In addition, during some weeks containers could be chosen to raise the question of whether a longer container always holds more. Making these kinds of estimations are often difficult for children in upper elementary grades, but engaging in these kinds of investigations in the early years could help children develop more complex thinking about the ways that capacity works.

Play Dough

Working with play dough provides another context in which children often naturally engage in comparisons of length as they roll the play dough into long snakes. In addition to encouraging these kinds of conversations, materials can be chosen to scaffold children's thinking. For example, sticks of different lengths could be made available for children to compare their snakes to. They could also use these sticks as targets to try to make a snake that is longer than a given stick. Scissors or plastic knives could be used to cut play dough snakes so they are the same length as a given stick.

Pretend Play Contexts

In many prekindergarten and kindergarten classrooms, teachers routinely change the pretend play center to promote different kinds of play (and to attract different children in the room). Some contexts are more likely to promote measurement play than others, and not always in expected ways. For example, upon initial consideration, it may seem that a kitchen would be likely to promote engagements with measurement because adults measure so frequently when cooking; however, the wooden and plastic foods that often stock pretend kitchens typically do not lend themselves to being measured in the ways that real foods do. However, when the center is organized as a doctor's office many opportunities for measurement naturally present themselves. Having a scale or even a large balance available to weigh dolls allows children to begin to consider the attribute of weight. In prekindergarten or kindergarten, it is not particularly important if children can read the scale correctly; however, it is helpful for them to have conversations about which doll is heavier, and to begin to be able to think about the attribute of weight as separate from that of height.

Children will probably also enjoy using measuring tapes to measure a doll's height or the circumference of the head, since they have experience with doctors taking their own measurements in these ways; however, they are unlikely to be able to interpret these measuring tools at this point. And, with some support, children may be interested in making a tower of unifix or snapping cubes to measure a doll's height. Even if they do not count the number of cubes, creating towers of different lengths to represent the heights of different dolls is a useful way of exploring length. Teachers can support these investigations by providing dolls of different weights and heights.

The goal of all of these comparison activities is to help children recognize and name the attributes of length, weight, and capacity, and to understand that many objects can be measured in relation to more than one of these attributes. When children have a solid understanding of these attributes, comparison activities become less valuable (Van de Walle, Karp, Bay-Williams, & Wray, 2007), and it becomes more important to help children start to think about the role of units in measurement.

PLAY THAT BUILDS
UNDERSTANDINGS OF UNITS

To measure the length of any object, a child must choose a unit of measure and then place units end-to-end along the length, which is called *iterating* (Stephan & Clements, 2003). Units could be any physical object as long as they are the same size and easily manipulated by the child. For example, plastic teddy bears, unifix cubes, cut-out foot prints, and wooden blocks could all be used as units of measure. Van de Walle, Karp, Bay-Williams, and Wray (2007) suggest that long, thin objects such as straws or toothpicks may be particularly helpful for children's initial experiences measuring length, because their shape emphasizes the attribute of length.

For prekindergarten and kindergarten children, many of the same play contexts that provided opportunities to compare the lengths of objects can be adapted to provide opportunities for children to build an understanding of units. In designing, supporting, and debriefing these play experiences, the goal is to make the concept of units explicit for children by drawing attention to the ways that different objects can be used to measure and represent length. So, rather than simply working with sticks, children could be encouraged to use straws or toothpicks to measure the lengths of their play dough snakes. Towers of cubes could be used to measure the length of the classroom, and teachers could show students how to measure the length of dolls with dominoes or other objects. In prekindergarten and kindergarten competence in doing these measures is not necessary; however, teachers can draw students' attention to gaps between units and engage in discussions about what this might mean for the measure. In addition, being careful with language during these engagements can help students come to realize that it is the space a unit takes up that matters when measuring, rather than the number of units one has. In other words, when children move toward using rulers, it is important that they recognize that they are not counting numbers, but counting the number of inch-long units that it takes to measure an object's length. By talking to students about their snake being "three straws long," rather than "3 straws, 1, 2, 3," teachers can begin to reinforce this idea.

PLAYFUL MEASUREMENT LESSONS
THAT SUPPORT THE USE OF STANDARD TOOLS

In 1st and 2nd grades, it is likely that children will be ready for more opportunities to engage with formal measurement using either nonstandard or standard measuring tools. At the same time, it is also likely that there will be fewer opportunities for daily play where students might encounter opportunities to measure in sensory tables, with play dough, or in pretend play centers. One way to meet children's need for play as well as to engage them in more complex measurement work is to design lessons that incorporate the spirit of play, by including intriguing materials and opportunities to experiment.

To learn about measuring units, children need to have many experiences laying units end to end to cover a distance. Much of this exploration can be done with informal units of measure. For example, baskets of various laminated animal footprints could be provided so that students use footprints of children, dogs, polar bears, lions, or elephants to measure the length and width of the room, tables, or doors. A poster could be provided for children to record their measures with the different footprints. After children have had many experiences measuring with different-sized prints, teachers could engage them in conversations about what they had to think about to measure correctly (going in a straight line, leaving no gaps, not overlapping) as well as in conversations about why measuring with different foot prints produced different numbers.

Teachers could also design lessons where children return to contexts in which they played in previous years, such as by engaging in measurement activities using standard or nonstandard units with dolls, play dough, or block towers. By framing measurement lessons around contexts with which children are already familiar and in which they have already explored some measurement concepts, teachers make it easier for children to draw on their previous knowledge to shape new understandings. This process can be repeated when formal measuring tools are introduced by giving children the opportunity to go back and measure the room with a yardstick, instead of footprints, or to measure a play dough snake with a ruler instead of unifix cubes. Returning to these play contexts connects the formal mathematics to children's informal experiences.

Helping children attend to measurement in the classroom requires that teachers see available opportunities for guiding children's thinking in these ways, rather than focusing only on counting and shape identification, which tend to be emphasized in early childhood contexts. For example, when children in the preschool classroom I observed played with chain link or link blocks, teachers regularly encouraged them to count how many links or blocks were in their chains or towers, but rarely asked them to compare the lengths of multiple towers or to use the towers or chains to measure the length of anything else in the classroom. However, by using these relatively simple prompts teachers could open up opportunities for children to explore additional strands of mathematics.

CHAPTER 7

The Mathematical Practices

The mathematical practices were included in the Common Core State Standards, along with the content standards, to direct educators' attention toward ways of thinking mathematically that extend throughout the grade levels. These thinking practices are important for mathematically proficient students, and highlight important skills needed to solve significant mathematical problems. When thinking about the formal language of the mathematical practices described in the CCSS, it is tempting to think that these particular standards must be meant for older children. It can be difficult to imagine that kindergartners can "attend to precision" or that 2nd-graders can "construct viable arguments and critique the reasoning of others"; however, mathematical play is actually a site rich with opportunities for children to engage in the mathematical practices because the problems in which students engage during play are not well-defined, carefully structured by an adult, or simplified for their grade level. When children decide to build symmetrical figures with blocks, weigh toys in buckets on a balance, or complete a puzzle, they set problems for themselves where attending to precision, reasoning abstracting, and persevering to solve problems matters.

Often these play contexts may be one of very few spaces in school when children try to solve problems that are not well-defined. Teachers can create environments that encourage children to construct and solve their own problems and can be intentional about attaching the language of the mathematical practices to the problem-solving work children do in play. Using the language of the mathematical practices with children is important not only because it can help children to develop mathematical vocabularies, but it can also help children come to think of themselves as "mathematics people." In other words, when children see their play labeled as mathematical, they come to think of themselves as the kind of people who enjoy and are successful at mathematics (Esmonde, 2009). Researchers in science have found that engagement with significant content in informal spaces is particularly important for children who come from low-income or minority families, because the kinds of inter-actions and speaking practices that go on during informal interactions are more likely to be similar to the way they talk and play at home (Enyedy & Mukhopadhyay, 2007); and therefore, less likely to produce conflicts between school science and mathematics and their broader sense of themselves in the world.

In addition, empirical research has demonstrated that the more open-ended the mathematical problems children engage with during play, the more the play contributes to the children's future mathematical performances. For example, Pepler and Ross (1981) found that chil-dren who played with open-ended toys (like blocks) performed better on assessments of problem-solving skills than children who played with closed materials (like puzzles), and in other assessments demonstrated more creativity than children who played with closed materials. We know that children engage in a variety of mathematics during routine play (Ginsburg, 2006); however, when thinking about promoting the mathematical practices, we need to focus on how to create opportunities for play that is as open and complex as possible.

WHAT DO THE PRACTICES LOOK LIKE IN THE EARLY GRADES?

Before thinking about how to promote the mathematical practices in play, we need to understand what the practices look like broadly in the early grades. While all of the practices can be enacted at any grade level, some are more relevant to young children's play than others. Below, the eight mathematical practices are described using the language of the CCSSM (National Governors Association Center for Best Practices, 2010, pp. 6–8), along with some examples of what enacting each prac-tice might look like in the earliest grades.

Make Sense of Problems and Persevere to Solve Them

Enacting this standard requires that students find ways to get started on mathematical problems. Students can be encouraged to "plan a solu-tion pathway rather than simply jumping into a solution attempt." In addition, while working on the problem, children have opportunities to "monitor and evaluate their progress and change course if necessary."

Play offers many opportunities for persevering to solve a problem as well as for reconsidering the path chosen. For example, children who have decided to build enclosures to house toy animals may find that they don't have enough blocks to create all of the fencing they need. Rather than giving up the project or accepting the open spaces, children could be encouraged to make a new plan for the fence using a variety of strategies. They might create a smaller enclosure, count the blocks needed and then count all of the available blocks to see if they will have enough to create the desired number of pens, or they might consider different shapes of blocks to see whether they can compose equivalent units to create more fencing. Through attention and low-key interventions, adults can encourage children to find solutions to their problems rather than giving up and can highlight the result when children do decide to persevere.

Reason Abstractly and Quantitatively

This practice highlights recording quantitative information in written formats, which young children are unlikely to do in play, even if they are capable of such recording in other contexts. However, this practice also includes creating a "coherent representation of the problem at hand," and moving between abstract and concrete contexts. In classrooms where children are encouraged to reflect on and report on their play to their classmates, opportunities for this kind of reasoning and representation can be created if students are asked to draw pictures of problems they engaged with during play. This could even be done as a way of soliciting advice from classmates about how to handle a particular problem. In addition, this practice requires "considering the units involved" and "attending to the meaning of quantities." Play with scales and balances offer opportunities for adults to engage children in reasoning quantitatively in this way. Children can be encouraged to think about why so many cotton balls balance out just one small plastic block. Making sense of this equality—give the differences in quantity—is a significant act of reasoning for young children.

Construct Viable Arguments and Critique the Reasoning of Others

This practice, which suggests that children "make conjectures and build a logical progression of statements to explore the truth of their conjectures," demands engagement with others. While this can happen in whole-group and small-group conversations in the classroom, the free-wheeling context of play creates many opportunities for children to offer conjectures and to have their conjectures critiqued by others. Many of these conjectures will not be mathematical—"An alligator could eat up your dog!"—but even so, voicing these theories and listening to the reasoning of peers in response gives children practice in making and evaluating evidence and arguments. Adults can support this by encouraging children to appeal to evidence when making claims, rather than simply urging students not to argue. In addition, play can support specifically mathematical conjectures, such as when two students work to complete a puzzle together and must negotiate the most productive strategies (e.g., sort by color or shape, do edges first, or attend to recognizable figures).

Model with Mathematics

This practice involves making connections between the formal systems of mathematics (numbers, graphing, equations) and situations in the real world. This is another practice that is unlikely to emerge naturally during play contexts; however, teachers could help children enact the practice during debriefings. For example, a classroom might keep track of how many children chose each center for a day and create a graph or an equation to represent these choices. This information could be used to make decisions about which centers are popular and which might need to be re-designed to make them more attractive.

Use Appropriate Tools Strategically

To be successful in mathematics, children must know when they need a mathematical tool, which tool is likely to be most helpful, and how to use the chosen tool. Play contexts can be important sites for young children to practice these skills, because, unlike in many school mathematics lessons, the tools have not been selected and modeled ahead of time by the teacher. Making sure that rulers, tape measures, calculators, counting blocks, number charts, balances, scales, and hundred's charts are available to children during play creates opportunities for children to engage with this practice. In addition, adults can look for opportunities for children to productively use these tools in their play and can suggest their use when appropriate. Teachers can also highlight when children use tools appropriately to encourage others to engage in the practice. Furthermore, conversations about why different kinds of measuring tools were chosen could make for interesting mathematical explorations during play debriefings.

Attend to Precision

This practice highlights using correct and appropriate mathematical language as well as paying attention to details when solving mathematical problems, such as choosing appropriate measurement units or clearly identifying where numbers come from in written problems and what they represent. Many young children have natural tendencies to be precise. They may, for example, write and rewrite their name until it looks the way they want it to, or they may meticulously trim their play dough to make it the same size as the cover of the play dough container, or they may fold and refold doll clothes so that the line of symmetry is as exact as possible. For the most part, teachers do not need to work very hard to create these opportunities for children during play; however, it is important that adults recognize these activities and name the child's desire to be precise as important mathematically. This can be done both in the moment and in debriefings afterward. In addition, teachers can make connections during formal mathematics lessons where precision is important to acts of precision that they observe children engaging in during play. In this way, more children can come to see themselves as mathematical.

Look For and Make Use of Structure

This practice includes recognizing and using patterns as well as other mathematical structures (such as recognizing that adding three blocks to seven blocks produces the same result as adding seven blocks to three blocks—and that this is also true for other sets of numbers). Sets of blocks provide many opportunities for children to investigate and make use of geometric structures. For example, in a set of wooden blocks, children may come to recognize that a particular blue rectangle unit can also be made by two green squares, four orange rectangles, or two yellow triangles. In addition, games and play sets that invite students to look for and create patterns can promote this practice. Again, teachers can both acknowledge these efforts when they occur, and also encourage investigations by offering challenges such as: How many different ways do you think we could build a road this long?

Look For and Express Regularity in Repeated Reasoning

This practice emphasizes recognizing patterns in calculations and in recognizing relationships between equations and graphical representations. Young children may have opportunities to begin to develop this practice when they recognize or produce patterns, but the practice will become more relevant to students as they become more mathematically proficient.

While students in the primary grades can, to some degree, engage in all of the mathematical practices described in the CCSSM, some practices are more meaningful for young students, particularly in play contexts. The next section provides descriptions of the ways that two of the most relevant mathematical practices emerge during play.

FOCAL PRACTICE 1:
MAKING SENSE OF PROBLEMS
AND PERSEVERING TO SOLVE THEM

One of the advantages regular play provides is the opportunity for children to linger over problems and to return to them day after day. Teachers can build on this opportunity by recognizing where rich mathematical problems are likely to occur in the classroom as well as by creating structures that help children to persevere. In thinking about supporting children's problem-solving efforts teachers can consider: the potential mathematics involved in the problem, the level of challenge for the particular child, interventions that might make the problem more challenging or might encourage the child to return to the problem in the future, and supports that might help the child record the work so that past thinking is not lost. Here are a couple of particular examples. As you read them, think about what you might do as a teacher to support students' perseverance with these activities as mathematical problems as well as play activities.

Example 1

During recess, 1st-graders Tondelia and Jessica are working together to build a house out of Lego blocks, using a picture that came with the building set as a model. They are struggling to make the roof come to a point in the center as it does in the picture, because Tondelia cannot find blocks that match those in the picture, while Jessica is building her side straight up. Both girls are starting to get frustrated and to argue about who gets to hold the picture and for how long. Recess will end in less than 5 minutes. What mathematics are the girls engaged with in this problem? What might you do as a teacher to encourage the girls to continue with the problem the next day?

Example 2

As part of a measurement unit, 2nd-graders are using rulers to measure objects around their desks. As children start to finish, the teacher says that the children can have 10 minutes to measure anything in the classroom. Jared decides he wants to measure how wide the classroom is; however, each time he picks up the ruler he loses track of where he put it down the previous time and he decides to just estimate the length by taking steps. What might you suggest to Jared that would encourage him to continue working on the problem he set for himself without taking over the thinking for him? What kind of mathematics would you want him to be thinking about as he worked on this problem?

Example 3

In center time, Ruby is working on a puzzle with many pieces. She is having difficulty figuring out how to put the pieces in and is trying each piece randomly. After a few moments, she pushes the puzzle aside and gets out one with fewer pieces that she has completed successfully many times before. Quickly, she takes the pieces out and puts them back in, and then does the same puzzle again. What might you do as a teacher to encourage Ruby to persevere in completing the more challenging puzzle? Why is it important mathematically that she develop the skills to solve more difficult puzzles?

All three examples provide children with opportunities to solve problems with significant mathematics. With the block building, the girls have the opportunity to get smarter about the 1st-grade geometry standard that asks students to compose 3-dimensional shapes to create a composite shape. In addition, because they are moving between a 2-dimensional and 3-dimensional representation, they have opportunities to strengthen their understandings of these different kinds of shapes. In the second example, Jared has opportunities to engage with multiple measurement standards: measuring lengths by selecting an appropriate tool, measuring a length twice using two different units, and estimating lengths. Finally, in working with the puzzle, Ruby can develop the skills she will need for the kindergarten geometry standards that ask students to analyze and compare 2-dimensional shapes and to compose simple shapes to form larger shapes. Clearly, all of these activities are not just play, but also mathematically worthwhile.

However, to emphasize the practice of perseverance, teachers need to find ways to encourage students to remain engaged in the problems they select for themselves even when they do not immediately see a solution strategy. For Tondelia and Jessica, this probably will mean helping them to develop strategies that will allow them to return to their work on the following day. First, it would be helpful to have a bin or a shelf where "in progress" block projects can be stored so that children don't feel they need to redo their previous work, and so that they come to learn that some projects and problems are too big for one session, but still solvable over time. Second, teachers can acknowledge the value of the girls' chosen task so that girls feel that it is worthwhile to continue and can articulate the hard work that the girls have already done, by pointing out what they have already accomplished. It may be tempting to tell the girls that they can build the house "however they want to," but this would significantly reduce the mathematical complexity of the task because they would no longer be working from a 2-dimensional model or trying to compose a particular figure. Reassuring the girls that their task is challenging, worthwhile, and solvable may motivate them to continue. Third, teachers could consider whether the materials for the task need to be augmented. For example, in this case, it might be helpful to have a second picture of the house for the girls to work with. Finally, having a classroom routine where children regularly share finished creations may motivate the girls to persevere because they will know they will have an opportunity to show off what they made.

To support Jared, a teacher might want to commend him on his estimation strategy, but also encourage him to think about ways to get a more exact measure (attending to precision). Rather than immediately suggesting a tool, which would take over some of the mathematical work for him, a teacher might encourage him to look around the room to see what he could find that would make measuring easier. Possibilities include a yardstick, a measuring tape, a second ruler that he could place down before he lifted the other up, a sentence strip to use for the same purpose, or a decision to measure the tiles on the floor and use those to count. The goal is not just to have Jared do the measuring, but to have him think through the challenge of measuring a long length and to figure out a possible solution strategy. Having mathematical tools present in the classroom and freely accessible to children will promote this kind of flexible thinking.

Ruby's engagement with the puzzle is typical of many children. Because they engage with puzzles only during play times, they never formally learn strategies for tackling more challenging puzzles, and thus, do not develop the spatial thinking skills that more complex puzzles would support. However, experiencing frustration when not being able to put together a puzzle is a valuable (and low stakes) way of learning how to manage feelings when solving a difficult problem. Ruby may benefit from some explicit instruction in puzzle-solving strategies (as discussed in Chapter 4), such as looking for parts of a picture across the shapes. In addition, she may need help choosing an appropriate puzzle for her. Perhaps she chose one that was too challenging in addition to one that was too easy. Although we want children to make choices during play, as teachers we want to help scaffold these choices so that they are more mathematically enriching, but also so they are more pleasurable. Children enjoy a "just right" challenge.

FOCAL PRACTICE 2:
ATTENDING TO PRECISION

The practice of attending to precision is about students learning to be exact in their mathematical problem solving, but also about learning to use vocabulary that accurately (and precisely) describes mathematical ideas. Often during play and informal mathematical engagements children have their own desires to be precise in the ways that they interact with the world. For example, during clean up, Carter set about creating sticks of unifix cubes that were exactly 8 cubes long, because that was the number of cubes that the teacher handed out when the class used the cubes to play Bingo. No teacher instructed him to make all of the sticks identical and it would have been faster to scoop the cubes into the bucket without making sticks at all; however, Carter sought to create order out of the chaos of the pile of blocks. He was so committed to this project that when other children joined him to help clean up, he instructed them to make sticks of eight and gave them some of the sticks he made so they could check their work against his.

Similarly, when many children fold blankets in housekeeping, they work hard to ensure that the edges of the blankets line up exactly before creating the next fold. In addition, many children working on pattern block puzzles will carefully align pieces so that they match the border exactly, and will seek out help from adults if they cannot achieve this on their own. That said, some children may have a "close enough is good enough" attitude. For these children, teachers can encourage attending to precision even during play as a way of developing children's abilities to both recognize and value exactness. For example, in the following interaction, the teacher stepped in to both frame a mathematical problem for the children and to encourage them to find an exact answer to the question they raised.

Kindergartners Ben and Jeremy were playing at the sensory table, scooping up lima beans and pouring them into buckets. Then Ben stopped, held up his bucket and said, "I got more than you." Jeremy looked in Ben's bucket and then held up his and said, "No, I got more than you." Seeking to get support for his position, Jeremy grabbed Dahlia's arm as she passed by, said to her, "Don't I got more beans than Ben?" Dahlia stopped, moderately interested, looked at the two buckets, and shrugged. At this point, Ms. Murphy intervened, and asked: "How could you find out which one of you really has more?" Dahlia answered, "You'd have to count them." At this point, Jeremy surreptitiously snuck his hand back into the table to grab more beans. Ms. Murphy suggested that both boys take their buckets to their table to count them, removing the temptation to add more beans. In addition, she dropped off some blank hundred's charts, and showed the boys how they could be used to organize their counting by putting one bean in each square. This frame helped them to create rows of ten and to keep track of the number of beans they had counted. In this interaction, Ms. Murphy not only communicated the idea that precision matters, but also generated a mathematical task (counting a large number) by pushing for an exact answer to the question the boys posed: who had the most beans?

In addition to counting and measuring carefully, attention to precision also means helping children to learn to use appropriate mathematical words. Unlike the tendency toward exactness, which many children enact without adult intervention, precision in vocabulary also requires teacher intervention because even adults use imprecise mathematical language much of the time. In particular, using proper language about labeling shapes, quantities of measurement, and large numbers can help children come to use these words easily and naturally. For example, when referring to the pattern blocks, making sure to talk about hexagons and trapezoids rather than the "yellow ones" and the "red ones" can help children to adopt precise mathematical language. Similarly, learning to say rhombus is not any more difficult than the word diamond, but children need adults to model this language if they are going to use it.

THE OTHER PRACTICES

Being aware of the other practices means that primary grades teachers can look for opportunities to highlight them when they come up. For example, ensuring that a variety of mathematical tools are easily accessible will encourage children to seek out and use tools appropriately, although teachers may need to remind children of what these tools can do and to model their use. Similarly, teachers can be on the lookout for when children are making mathematical arguments—for example, what holds more, which is bigger, what shapes count as "the same"—and can support children in making their own arguments and in listening and responding to the arguments of others. Broadly, the goal of the mathematical practices is to help children not just "know" math, but to think and act in mathematical ways. Because they are open-ended and filled with problems that matter to children, play contexts provide ideal spaces for children to engage in these kinds of inquiries.

Part III

MAKING FORMAL
LESSONS PLAYFUL

CHAPTER 8

Designing Formal Lessons That Build on Play

Although a lot of mathematical learning can occur during children's free play—particularly with thoughtful teacher interventions—formal lessons provide opportunities for teachers to target particular mathematical objectives by leveraging the experiences children have during play (NAEYC & NCTM, 2002). One of the advantages of having regular time for play at school is that teachers can closely observe play to see what experiences children are having that can be drawn into informal lessons. Another advantage is that teachers can seed the play environment to try to promote kinds of play that will provide important foundations for future learning experiences. During formal lessons, teachers can make links to play through a variety of strategies, including mathematizing the language of play, assigning tasks that are designed on children's play experiences, and designing formal lessons that embody some of the characteristics of play.

MATHEMATIZING THE LANGUAGE OF PLAY

Mathematical symbols and language work to create connections between abstract ideas like *the number two* and experiences in the real world like holding *two cookies* (which is preferable to holding one cookie). As children make more and more of these connections, their understanding of each abstract mathematical idea becomes richer (for example, the number 2 can be used to talk about cookies, people, age, order, etc.). Mathematizing requires that children "take situations and problems from the world around them and formulate them in mathematical terms" (NRC, 2009, p. 44). During formal lessons, teachers can help children connect mathematical language, symbols, and tools to their experiences during play. By doing so, teachers make it possible for children to make more sense of the target mathematics.

To illustrate the way that rich connections between experiences and mathematical ideas can deepen student understanding, I present two episodes taken from 2nd-grade classrooms during introductions to units on linear measurement. In both cases, the teachers attempt to make connections between real-world experiences and the mathematics under discussion. However, in the first case, the children have not had opportunities to engage in free play in the classroom so the teacher has to bring in a real-world context from her own experiences to frame the discussion. In the second case, the teacher elicits comments from students based on her observations during center time, which she schedules each week on Friday afternoon for 45 minutes.

Episode One

Ms. Freckman, a beginning 2nd-grade teacher, gathered her 18 children around her on the carpet. She asked them to imagine that they lived a long time ago and needed to buy wood for a fire.

> *Ms. Freckman:* How do you make sure . . . how do you make sure you're getting as much wood as you're supposed to? What do you measure it with? *[Four of the eighteen students raised their hands and Ms. Freckman called on Emily.]*
> *Emily:* Paperclips.
> *Ms. Freckman:* Okay. How else could you measure if you didn't have paperclips. If you didn't have metal? *[Two of the eighteen students raised their hands. Ms. Freckman called on Dhruv.]*
> *Dhruv:* A TV. *[Several students laughed.]*
> *Ms. Freckman:* How could you measure with a TV? *[Ms. Freckman wanted the children to think about using their hands to measure, which would be the focus of the lesson. She pulled on a real-world scenario where she knew this was done.]*
> *Ms. Freckman:* Who knows how they measure horses? *[Three children raised their hands. Ms. Freckman called on Peyton.]*
> *Peyton:* You can measure with fingers.
> *Ms. Freckman:* You could. That's interesting. Allie, how do you measure horses? *[Allie did not raise her hand, but Ms. Freckman knew she played "horses" on the playground.]*

Samanatha: On a scale?

Ms. Freckman: No, not on a scale. When I buy a horse I ask how many hands it is. They take their hands and they start down at the horse's hoof and they go 1, 2, 3, 4 *[pantomined measuring with her hands]*. We're going to use our hands to measure today.

In this episode, four of eighteen children spoke and only six of the eighteen children in the classroom raised their hands. The children who did speak struggled to participate competently in the conversation about the mathematics. There are many reasons for this, but a major issue is that the contexts drawn on for the mathematical conversations were unfamiliar to students. Initially, they were supposed to imagine what it was like a long time ago; however, when asked for an available measurement tool, Emily suggested paperclips. This was not what Ms. Freckman had in mind—both because it would not have been any more available long ago than rulers and because the intended measurement tool of the day was hands. However, Emily was familiar with paperclips as perhaps the most common measurement tool substituted for rulers in elementary classrooms and so offered this answer. In contrast to Emily, Dhruv, a student less adept at the school game, and perhaps more interested in making classmates laugh than in getting praise for a correct answer, offered a "TV" as a possibility. Over time, if students learn that they will not be able to participate competently in mathematical classroom discussions, they often seek other kinds of validation in the classroom—such as by becoming the class comedian.

Ms. Freckman, who realized that the conversation was not going as intended, tried to redirect the children to a context that promoted thinking about hands as measuring tools. However, the children, less familiar with the procedures of measuring a horse than she, suggested fingers and scales as possible measuring tools. While both these tools are reasonable objects with which to measure, they were not the correct answer and Ms. Freckman was forced to answer her own question.

As a result, at the end of this episode, fewer than one-third of the children participated in any way in the conversation, and none of the children who spoke felt that they had participated competently. In addition, it is unlikely that the conversation deepened children's understanding of measurement because the contexts drawn on were so unfamiliar to them, and they could not make connections between the mathematical ideas and the real-world scenario. As a teacher, Ms. Freckman knew that she needed to make connections to her children's experiences and said after the lesson that she had raised the context of measuring horses because she knew several girls in the class loved the animals. However, a child's fascination or fantasy about horses does not necessarily provide the rich experiences needed to understand a mathematics problem. In addition, even if the girls most enamored of horses had been able to answer the problem, the majority of the children still would have been left without opportunities to make connections. Similarly, even if another more common context had been drawn on—such as cooking—Ms. Freckman would not have known which of her children had had relevant experiences and which would need other kinds of connections to be made.

Episode Two

The following episode comes from the classroom of a more experienced teacher, who has spent a significant amount of time studying her own teaching in learning communities with colleagues and who was committed to provide some time for play each week in her 2nd-grade class. In the month before she began the measurement unit, she added a measurement center to the play options for her classroom that included rulers, tape measures, balances, scales, yardsticks, unifix cubes, containers, and objects to measure. In addition, she encouraged as many students as possible to explore those materials. She then drew on these experiences in her introduction to her measurement unit.

> *Mrs. James:* Raise your hand if you've ever measured something.
> *[Mrs. James waited as hands went up. Twenty out of twenty-two students raised their hands.]*
> *Mrs. James:* Devon, your hand's not up. You never measured something? What about here in the classroom?
> *Devon:* We measured our desks.
> *Mrs. James:* Last week with Evan, right? So put your hand up.
> *[Akira, who also hadn't raised her hand, put it up.]*
> *Mrs. James:* Let's write down some of the things you measured. *[She went around the room calling on each child to name the object. Some children said "He took mine," but she had them say their object anyway. At the end of 3 minutes every child had spoken and 14 objects were listed on the board.]*

Mrs. James: Wow. That's a lot to have measured. Now, I have another question for you. What did you measure with? Tell your neighbor what you used to measure. *[Most children leaned to talk to their neighbor. Two or three sit silently.]* Okay so here are some things I heard.

Mrs. James wrote down "ruler," "measuring tape," and "yard stick" in one column; "unifix cubes," "paper, clips" and "teddy bears" in the middle column; and "hands," "feet," and "fingers" in a third column. She continued the discussion by engaging the children in a conversation about what is different about the things in each of the columns, focusing on issues of standard and nonstandard measurement.

Mrs. James did a lot in this episode to encourage the participation of all of her students. First of all, rather than offering her own context for measurement, she asked the children to think of a time they had measured something. Because she made measurement tools available to the children during center time, and she had observed how the tools were used, she was confident that all of the children had some experience with measuring. As a result, she was able to prompt Devon when he did not raise his hand in response to her question, and by mentioning the experience at school, she reminded Akira, who also had not raised her hand, to think about what she might have done in the previous weeks. Using play as a regular context for mathematical experimentation not only provided children with experiences that will help them understand the lesson, but also provided a structure where Mrs. James could begin the mathematics lesson with every child offering a correct answer.

Later, she asked students to tell their neighbor what they used to measure. This participation move also serves a couple of purposes. First, it provided an opportunity for a different kind of speech so students who do not like to talk in front of the classroom could get a chance to talk. In addition, it also provided some variety in the lesson, reducing the likelihood that the children would get bored. This process also allowed the children to begin to mathematize their experiences by attaching language to something they did in another context in relation to a mathematics lesson. By naming object measured, the children could begin to think about what kinds of attributes are measurable and how to talk about them, since many children did not just name what they measured, but also described how they went about it.

Second, by writing down things that she heard, Mrs. James represented the ideas in a new way, validated student responses, and also created some wiggle room for herself as a teacher. She knew that she would like to put the following on the board: a ruler, objects used to measure that all have the same size, and objects used to measure that all have different sizes. This sort of organization would allow her to open a conversation with students about units of measure and to do some exploration of what happens when people use nonstandard measures. By asking students to whisper to each other and then selecting answers for the board, Mrs. James ensured that she could get all of the kinds of responses she needed on the list without having to get the children to "guess" the right answer she had in mind. If she did not hear an answer necessary to the classification scheme she was setting up, she could add it to the list on the board without fuss.

By creating the chart, Mrs. James made a representation in written language of children's measurement experiences in play that could be used to help the children build the big idea of the differences between standard and nonstandard measures. Seeing the measurement tools organized in such a way encouraged the students to think about similarities and differences within the context of this lesson. More broadly, it taught the children that mathematical ideas could be organized in a written chart, and that such a representation is a useful tool for making connections between ideas.

Overall, Mrs. James designed an opening to her measurement unit that explicitly sought to attach mathematical language to the informal measurement experiences that her children have had in school and at home. Although the time her students spent interacting with the measurement tools she provided during play was valuable, mastery of 2nd-grade measurement ideas requires that the students can talk about units of measure, name measurement tools, and describe attributes to be measured. Formal lessons that focus on mathematical language are essential for this purpose and are far more meaningful if that language can be attached to experiences children have had. Providing time for mathematical play in the classroom ensures that all children will bring relevant experiences to the lesson, rather than only those children who have had experiences similar to the teacher's. Although Mrs. James' opening was relatively simple, it required long-term thoughtful planning on her part in order to ensure that children had plenty opportunities to engage with the measurement tools before the formal lesson.

ASSIGNING TASKS BASED ON STUDENT EXPLORATIONS

Often in a classroom where play occurs regularly, a student or group of students will become engaged in a task that has rich mathematical possibilities. However, even with encouragement from the teacher during planning and debriefing, other children may not choose to take up the task. It is important that choice time be protected as a part of the day when children can make decisions about what they will do—particularly given how few opportunities most children have to make choices in schools today—however, teachers can import valuable tasks from play into formal mathematics lessons and then require that all children engage with the task.

Observation and even some note-taking can support this process. Although it is important to make connections between children's play and their work in formal mathematics, it is probably not ideal to let the mathematical topic each day be guided by whatever happened during play the day or the week before. Research has demonstrated that when preschool teachers address mathematics only when it arises during children's play, then little mathematics tends to get done in either formal or informal environments because literacy activities tend to dominate (Ginsburg, Lee, & Boyd, 2008; Graham, Nash, & Paul, 1997). As with older children, preschool children benefit from a systematic introduction to mathematical concepts (NRC, 2009). Recently, a number of strong curricula for preschool children have been published, including *Big Math for Little Kids* (Ginsburg, Greenes, & Balfanz, 2003) and "Building Blocks for Early Childhood Mathematics" (Sarama & Clements, 2004), which could be used to plan and structure mathematics lessons across the year. For children in the other primary grades, it is likely that standards and curricula are already in place. Rather than routinely disrupting planned activities to focus on problems generated during play, teachers can take notes about problems and plan to use them when appropriate for particular units. These problems can be introduced by showing pictures of what children did, by asking children to talk about the problem they encountered, or simply by telling a story about what was observed.

Initially note-taking could occur simply by taking a picture of the problem or by jotting down a quick description on a post-it note that could be attached to the appropriate page in the written curriculum. Then, at the appropriate time the problem could be developed into a formal lesson. Figure 8.1 shows one possible way of creating such a lesson plan; however, any standard planning format would also work. Below is a description of how one teacher took a problem she observed students pose during play and how she adapted it for a formal lesson a few weeks later.

Ms. Chang, a kindergarten teacher, noticed during play time that Cory built a "road" out of blocks. In doing so, he used a variety of blocks to make rectangular units, including two squares, four small rectangles, and two triangles. Ms. Chang took a picture of this student's work on her digital camera to document the ways that he was composing and decomposing shapes. She was happy that this student was working on this kindergarten geometry standard during play, but wanted to deepen the learning for him and other students. In going back to the CCSSM she identified two content standards she wanted to focus on in a teacher-directed activity:

Figure 8.1. Lesson Plan Template

Lesson Topic:

Standard(s):

Connection to lesson in curriculum:

Problem in play:

Modifications for lesson:

Materials: Estimated time:

Formative assessment/Attend to:

- Compose simple shapes to form larger shapes.
- Correctly name shapes regardless of their orientations or overall size.

In addition, Ms. Chang saw an opportunity to highlight the practice standard "Construct viable arguments and critique the reasoning of others." Ms. Chang saved the picture to use during the opening of her Shapes geometry unit. She planned a 3-day lesson based on the problem. On the first day, she showed the children the picture of Cory's road and invited him to talk about what he had done. She then asked the children to describe what they noticed, which allowed her to make sure that all of the children heard the appropriate vocabulary to describe the shapes in the picture. Using her interactive white board, Ms. Chang drew rectangles around each unit, showing the children how the road was made up of four rectangles that had been composed in different ways. She then gave sets of blocks to pairs of children and invited them to make rectangles the same size as Cory's in as many different ways as they could. In putting together the sets of blocks, she included all of the ones that Cory had used as well as some that he had not, such as smaller triangles. As she moved around the room while students were working, Ms. Chang made an effort to name the shapes that each pair was using. She also was on the look-out for a pair that made a rectangle using a variety of shapes, (such as two small triangles and one square). After about 10 minutes of exploration, she asked all of the students individually to draw one way that they had made a rectangle with blocks. During sharing time, Ms. Chang invited students sitting in the circle to show their pictures and describe what they had drawn. This provided students with an opportunity to attach appropriate language to the blocks they had used.

On the second day, Ms. Chang posed a new problem to her students. She asked them to try to find all of the ways to compose the large rectangular unit with the blocks they had. She asked student pairs to draw pictures of each "way" they found, to talk with their partners about what made the new way different, and to figure out how they knew when they had them all. She thought that these prompts, particularly the last two, would provide students with the opportunity to construct arguments and critique the reasoning of others. For example, when one pair got into an argument about whether a unit that was constructed with two small triangles first and then a square was the same as or different than a unit with a square followed by two identical small triangles, she encouraged the pair to remember this discussion so that they could bring it to the large group. At the end of the lesson, Ms. Chang put students' posters at the front of the room, and led the class in a discussion of whether they thought they could be sure that they had found all of the ways. She guided them toward thinking about ways to represent their work that would keep it organized to allow for students to see if all possible combinations could be found. She also supported students in having a conversation about what counts as "different" in mathematics.

On the third day, Ms. Chang planned a short assessment activity, where she gave each student a set of paper blocks and asked the children to make all of the rectangular units possible when using at least one square. She also had the students write labels for each of the blocks they used. In this set of lessons, Ms. Chang was able to bring a problem a child created during play into the formal mathematics lesson. In doing so, she created a series of lessons that addressed the CCSSM and actively engaged the students. This resulted in all of the students being able to build the geometric skills that students who routinely play with blocks get to work on routinely. In addition, it re-energized play around blocks during free time, leading to both more children choosing to play with blocks, and more mathematical language being used in that play. Creating connections between play and formal mathematics promoted more learning than would have been possible in either unsupported play or in formal lessons taken strictly from a curriculum guide. In the beginning, it may be difficult to identify productive play activities to draw on for lessons. Appendices A and B, which list play contexts where mathematics frequently arises and language that is usually used in mathematical ways, may help you to identify play problems in your classroom.

INTRODUCING PLAYFULNESS INTO THE FORMAL CURRICULUM

In some classrooms, particularly in the later primary grades, regular time for play may not be practical, given constraints imposed by the district or school. While teachers can still advocate for their children by lobbying for changes in formal policies and by finding time for play before the bell in the morning or during rainy day recesses, teachers can also find ways to make their formal lessons more playful as a way of making mathematics both more enjoyable and more engaging for children. In addition, making mathematics lessons more playful can also provide children with some of the opportunities for discovery and problem solving that regular play would provide. Going back to Burghardt's (2011) definition of play, true play is:

- Pleasurable
- Light-hearted (not serious)
- Repeated
- Engaged in without stress
- Freely chosen

In addition, play often includes:

- Opportunities for social engagement
- Creative thinking
- Use of materials that are appealing
- Physical movement
- Imagination

Obviously, a playful lesson will not be able to embody all of these characteristics. In particular, in a lesson, children are not able to choose what they will do or for how long they will do it. In addition, children may not be able to choose whom they work with or the materials they use, although teachers might certainly consider introducing opportunities for children to make some choices within lessons as a part of creating a more playful atmosphere. Creating lessons that are pleasurable, light-hearted, and stress-free should be the focus of designing a playful learning space. In addition, teachers can think about purposeful ways of using toys that might commonly be used in play—either in the classroom or in other contexts—as the focus of the lessons.

The questions in Figure 8.2 offer a place for teachers to begin brainstorming playful lessons while working off either a formal curriculum or a set of standards.

Here are two examples at different grade levels of how a playful lesson might be designed working off of either one of the CCSS or a lesson in a published curricula.

Figure 8.2. Questions to Reflect on When Adapting Curriculum and Standards for Playful Lessons

1. How could the standard or lesson be changed to allow for some student choice?

2. How could interactions among children during the lesson be fostered?

3. What materials that children might enjoy working with could be used to teach the lesson?

4. How might the lesson be changed or adapted to allow for multiple pathways or creative solutions?

5. How might a context that is pleasurable or engaging to children be meaningfully invoked in the lesson?

6. In what ways could stress be reduced in the lesson?

7. How could the lesson be deepened and extended so that children could build on their experiences over time?

A Kindergarten Example

In kindergarten there are a variety of standards related to counting and cardinality. For example, during kindergarten, children are expected to:

- K.CC.B.4.A. Say the number names in the standard order, pairing each object with one and only one number name and each number name with one and only one object.
- K.CC.B.4.B. Understand that the last number name said tells the number of objects counted. The number of objects is the same regardless of their arrangement or order in which they are counted.
- K.CC.B.4.5. Count to answer "how many?" questions about as many as 20 things arranged in a line, a rectangular array, or a circle, or as many as 10 things in a scattered configuration; given a number from 1–20, count that many objects.

There are many activities that could be used to help children develop these skills; however, regardless of the chosen activity, children will need repeated opportunities to develop these skills. As a result this content makes for a productive site to introduce play into the curriculum as a way of making the activities more engaging for children so they will be more likely to repeat them. In thinking about the characteristics of play, the features of choice, engaging materials, and social interactions seem like easy aspects of play to incorporate into designing lessons for this mathematical content. Take a moment to consider how you might do this.

One way might be to put together a series of buckets of plastic bags, each with different kinds of activities in them that address the focal standards. Then over the course of a week, children could make choices about which activities they would like to engage in for 20 minutes at a time. By allowing children to choose activities, rather than rotating them through centers, teachers can invoke a more playful spirit in the classroom. If all of the activities are designed to address the target standards, then it does not matter if some children return to the same activity each day while others try something new. Teachers might also think about ways to incorporate activities that children generally enjoy, like art, building, or game play into these activities. Here are some possibilities for these standards:

- Grab a handful of puffballs, beads, sequins, etc., and glue on a piece of paper to make a picture. Count how many objects are on the paper. Write that number on the paper and then make a second picture with *exactly* the same number of objects.
- Provide a bag or box of different colored cars, dinosaurs, fruit, or other objects. Have children work together in pairs to count how many of each one there are. Provide a recording sheet for children to write down their answers.
- Count out 18 blocks of any kind. Make the tallest tower you can with those 18 blocks. Try again. See if you can use different blocks or rearrange them to make a taller tower with 18 blocks.
- Play any linear board game. Use two 1–6 dice to roll.
- Use plastic animal counters to build a zoo with blocks. Draw a picture of the zoo and write down how many of each kind of animal are in each pen. Trade pictures with a friend and build each other's zoos.
- Work with a partner to make as many collections of 20 objects as you can. Take a digital picture of your work.
- Take turns with a partner arranging a collection of 12 objects in different ways. Which arrangements are easiest to count? When you decide, ask the teacher for a larger collection to count.

- Give partners a small collection of Lego blocks. Have one partner build a structure behind a folder used as a divider. The first partner should describe the structure to the second partner, saying how many of each kind of block were used in what ways to see if the second partner can build an identical structure. Then switch.
- Create a collection of interesting objects in jars (shells, marbles, beads, etc.) with amounts from 1–25. Invite students to count the amounts in each jar. Write the answer on the side in dry erase marker and order from least to greatest. Children should erase numbers on jars when finished.

Obviously additional activities—based on the materials available in your classroom—could be created, and while it would take some time and planning to design and organize these activities, once they have been designed, no additional planning work would be needed throughout the week. In addition, many curriculum guides have activities that could be easily adapted for this setting, and some activities may be able to be stored intact from year to year, making planning in future years even easier.

A 2nd-Grade Example

The lesson in Figure 8.3 is a relatively typical measurement lesson, in which children first use the rulers in their math books and then on objects. There are a number of ways to make a lesson like this more playful, including simply increasing the number of objects students can measure and allowing for some student choice about what to measure. Students could also engage in measurement activities outside, which could generate curiosity about the natural world and allow for some challenging measurement work as students try to measure very long lengths.

Mr. Hodges, a 2nd-grade teacher, made his lesson on linear measurement more playful by introducing an imaginative context to his class. He encouraged them to think about what would happen if a magic spell were put on their class, causing them all to grow twice as tall as they were. After the children pondered some of the consequences of this, he asked the students to work with a partner to make a model of each person twice as tall as their current height on butcher paper. He also provided a variety of measurement and drawing tools to get this done,

Figure 8.3. 2nd-Grade Sample Lesson

How would you adapt the lesson below to make it more playful?

Standards:

Measure the length of an object by selecting and using appropriate tools such as rulers, yard sticks, meter sticks, and measuring tapes.

Estimate lengths using units of inches, feet, centimeters, and meters.

Warm Up:

Model use of ruler with inches and centimeters, yard stick, meter stick, and tape measure for children.

Independent Practice:

Worksheet:

Problems 1–8: Circle the appropriate measuring tool for each pictured object.

Problems 9–15: Use a ruler to measure the pictured objects in either centimeters or inches.

Problems 16–18: Measure the length of your desk, your math book, and your shoe.

---

and encouraged students to think about what would happen to their body parts such as their arms, legs, feet, and heads. This problem was playful because it encouraged the children to enter an imaginary world, to work with each other, to create a creative product, and to engage with a problem that could be solved in multiple ways.

The problem was mathematical because it asked children to make important measurement decisions. For example, they decided to measure in inches or centimeters not based on directions from the book, but focused on the mathematical constraints of the problem. Some students used centimeters because they decided it would give a more exact measurement, while other students chose to use inches because this would produce smaller numbers that would be easier to work with. All of these decisions could be discussed after the work period. In addition, the problem provided many opportunities to measure since students not only measured many parts of their bodies, but also used the measuring tools to draw their figures on the paper, often needing to re-measure and confirm each other's measurements. The problem also raised opportunities for estimation as students talked about how close was "close enough." In short, this problem not only made mathematics a more pleasurable and enjoyable part of the day, but also made the intellectual content of the problem richer. Introducing play into mathematics lessons should not be seen in opposition to promoting rigor, but as supporting it. Of course, all lessons will not contain aspects of play, but as children move through the primary grades and have fewer and fewer opportunities for play, finding ways to bring choice, excitement, movement, imagination, and curiosity into formal lessons becomes more and more important.

CHAPTER 9

Including Play
in Assessments

Teachers have always had to find ways to document what the students in their classes have been learning; however, since 2001, assessment, even in the early schooling years, has become a more high-stakes endeavor for both teachers and children. Although children before Grade 3 may not have to take formal tests of their mathematical abilities, many school districts may require standard quarterly assessments, and as publicly funded preschools expand, many of these programs are also including mandates for assessment. In addition, many school districts are asking teachers to make increasingly detailed reports about children's mathematical and literacy knowledge, with some districts requiring teachers to complete written forms that require teachers to make judgments about 20–50 discrete skills for each child. Seeing play as a context in which assessment can occur has the potential to both reduce anxiety during the assessment for children and also provide teachers with more contexts in which they can observe particular skills. In addition, performing assessments under more natural conditions can provide more accurate pictures of what children can do mathematically. Hirsh-Pasek, Kochanoff, Newcombe, and de Villiers argued that "it would be wise to develop instruments that examined language, literacy, mathematics, and social skills as they were used in everyday situations" (2005, p. 11) in order to identify important learning processes as well as discrete knowledge and skills. Seeing children use a skill in context often provides more information than seeing them use the same mathematics in isolation.

Teachers in K–2 classrooms are likely to be already mired in assessment protocols and requirements; however, they may be able to reduce demands on themselves and their children by looking for informal contexts in which some assessments may be performed or by designing (or redesigning) assessment tasks so that they feel more playful. In addition, teachers may find it helpful to go back to the mathematical standards for their grade level to reflect on what it is that children are supposed to know and do. *Backward Design*, the practice of looking at learning goals in order to develop assessments (Wiggins & McTighe, 2005), has been widely used for some years; however, with the increasing number of decisions about assessments being made at the district, state, or national level, fewer teachers are developing their own assessments and making explicit connections to the standards. Returning to the CCSSM for a target grade level and thinking about them within the context of assessment *and* play might help teachers think about how assessments could be productively modified to either take place during play or have elements of play introduced into the assessment. Questions to consider include:

- Which aspects of the assessment are observational? How can I create spaces in my classroom that will elicit the target skills or vocabulary in play settings?
- Which aspects of the assessment can be implemented as performance tasks and how might these tasks incorporate aspects of play?
- What role is there for social interaction in the assessments (perhaps either before or after) and how could that social interaction occur in a playful setting?
- In what ways might there be space for revising written assessments so that they draw on contexts that are familiar to children in play?

Prekindergarten teachers may find themselves facing similar requirements for assessment or they may find themselves having the opposite problem: being offered very little guidance in terms of what to assess in mathematics or how to do it. This is particularly true because the CCSSM do not describe appropriate mathematics for preschoolers, although many states have early learning standards, which could be productively used for designing assessments, even if they were produced in other contexts. (Those for Georgia are shown in Figure 9.1.) Many of these standards could be productively assessed during play contexts, while others could be assessed in targeted activities that drew on familiar play activities for children. The following sections will describe both strategies for assessing

Figure 9.1. Georgia Early Learning and Development Standards

Number and Quantity	Measurement and Comparison	Geometry and Spatial Thinking	Mathematical Reasoning
Recites numbers up to 20 in sequence.	The child will explore and communicate about distance, weight, length, height and time.	Uses appropriate directional language to indicate where things are in their environment: positions, distances, order.	Estimates using math-ematical terms and understands how to check the estimate.
Recognizes numerals and uses counting as part of play and as a means for determining quantity.	Uses mathe-matical terms to describe experiences involving measurement.	Uses deliberate manipulation and describes process for fitting objects together.	Uses simple strategies to solve mathematical problems and communi-cates how he/she solved it.
Matches numerals to sets of objects with the same number, 0–10.	Compares objects using two or more attributes, such as length, weight and size.	The child will explore, recognize and describe shapes and shape concepts.	Uses reasoning skills to determine the solution to a mathematical problem and communi-cates why.
Describes sets as having more, less, same as/equal.	Uses a variety of techniques and standard and nonstandard tools to measure and compare length, volume (capacity) and weight.	Recognizes and names common two-dimensional and three-dimensional shapes, their parts and attributes.	
Quickly recognizes and names how many items are in a set of up to four items.			
Tells numbers that come before and after a given number up to 10.			
Matches two equal sets using one-to-one correspon-dence and understands they are the same.			
Counts at least 10 objects using one-to-one correspondence	Associates and describes the passage of time with actual events.	Combines simple shapes to form new shapes.	
Practices combining, separating and naming quantities.			
Describes data from classroom graphs using numerical math language.			
With adult guidance and when counting, understands and can respond with the last number counted to rep-resent quantity (cardinality).			

Note: Available at www.gelds.decal.ga.gov

mathematics through observation of play and strategies for designing assessments that draw on play. Prekindergarten and kindergarten contexts will be discussed separately from Grades 1 and 2 because the expectations for assessment are often so different across these grade levels.

ASSESSMENT THROUGH OBSERVATION

The writing of anecdotal records in both literacy and mathematics instruction is a long-standing practice in early grades education, and research has shown that teachers who regularly take notes on children's mathematical thinking become more interested in children's thinking and are able to ask questions that help children to describe their solution strategies instead of simply articulating correct answers (Borko, Mayfield, Marion, Flexer, & Cumbo, 1997). Traditionally, teachers have used a variety of strategies for recording and keeping track of these notes. For example, teachers have taken notes on sticky labels, which can then be organized in spiral notebooks with a page for each student, have written on notecards, which can be stored in divided boxes, and have used clipboards with forms that guide observations, which can be stored in student-specific folders (Smith, 2006). Appendix C shows one example of a teacher-made observational assessment form. New technologies have also created new possibilities for recording and storing. For example, electronic tablets can be used to record pictures as well as texts about student work. These notes can then be organized in a variety of ways. Apps like Evernote allow teachers to organize a variety of texts, notes, and photographs tagged for each student. Notes could also be sent directly to teachers' email accounts for cutting and pasting into other documents or sharing with parents. Similarly, social apps, like Instagram, can also be used with private accounts that can be accessed only by the classroom teacher or by the teacher and parents if desired. Instagram supports the organizing and sharing of photographs and captions, which can be helpful both because so much information can be captured through visual images and because taking the pictures takes much less time than writing notes. In addition to these widely available applications, a number of specifically designed educational software programs are available for doing this work.

The earlier chapters of this book provide examples of where particular mathematical content may emerge during play; however, when focused on assessment teachers may wish to promote certain materials or centers as a way of capturing engagements around particular mathematical ideas. Depending on what teachers would like to assess (e.g., which students engage with which materials or the ability of all students to identify sets of more or less), teachers can either allow students to decide whether they will interact with the focus materials or can ask that all students play in a particular center some time throughout the week.

Ideas for Assessing Mathematics in Play in Prekindergarten and Kindergarten

In thinking about assessing mathematical skills and knowledge during play, preschool and kindergarten teachers can consider two strategies for guiding their observations. The first is to identify particular children and to observe them over time for any kinds of mathematics in which they might engage. The second is to choose a mathematically-rich area of the room and focus observations on whichever children choose to interact with that area. For teachers new to observing mathematics in play the second strategy might be more productive because it will support learning about the kinds of mathematics that occurs in the room and refine skills for recognizing it. Appendix A, which lists the mathematical skills and concepts frequently observed with particular classroom materials, might be helpful in deciding where to begin observations. Writing descriptions or taking pictures of mathematical play can enrich knowledge gained from more formal assessments of mathematical learning. For example, observation might show strategies children use for grouping large numbers of objects for counting. Some children may not attempt to organize objects at all, while others may make rows or use sorting strategies to keep track of the count, and still others might organize groups of a particular size, such as 5 or 10 to make counting easier. All of these strategies provide insight into a child's knowledge of counting. Teachers may find it easiest to take notes in an open-ended format, but Appendix C provides an example of an observation form that can be used to guide notetaking if desired. Such forms could also provide support for parents, paraprofessionals or student teachers to take anecdotal records if desired.

In addition to observing the mathematics that occurs in toys chosen regularly in the classroom, teachers can also introduce new toys to draw out particular mathematical skills. For example, after teaching some focused mathematics lessons related to shape names and composing and decomposing of geometric figures, a new set of pattern block puzzles could be introduced as a toy for center time. Watching children complete the puzzles provides an opportunity to see if they use shape names to describe the blocks in another context and to see where they are in terms of seeing the relationship between shapes. For example some children may place the blocks into the puzzles using trial and error while others may make systematic choices looking at the sizes of blocks or the shape of the angles. Observing this work during play provides the opportunity to see what children can do without adult direction.

While observing play for purposes of mathematical assessment, teachers may also want to ask children questions to figure out more about what children understand and can do. Beginning with open-ended questions, such as "Can you tell me about what you made?" or "How did you figure that out?" allows children to start by pointing out what is important to them and to use the vocabulary that is dominant in their thinking. For example, a child who has been sorting blocks may not have been thinking about finding all of the small rectangles, but instead about finding all of the blue blocks. More focused questions can be used in follow up to assess children's mathematical understandings more thoroughly. For example, asking "How many more than Jared do you have?" may elicit an opportunity to observe counting strategies that wouldn't be present otherwise. However, when asking focused questions, take care to move beyond asking children to count the objects before them or to name shapes. These questions get asked frequently to young children by adults concerned with identifying mathematics in play, often well beyond the point at which they are useful for assessment. For example, once a teacher knows that all children can count collections up to 10 and name shapes, then asking students to do these things serves little purpose. Instead, questions should be asked to assess (and encourage) more advanced mathematical skills. Figure 9.2 offers the opportunity to practice assessing early number knowledge based on an observation of play.

Ideas for Assessing Mathematics in Play in 1st and 2nd Grades

In 1st- and 2nd-grade classrooms where teachers provide regular time for play as part of the regular school day, all of the strategies described in the previous section can be used, although the mathematics may be

Figure 9.2. Try It Out

During center time in a prekindergarten class, Jeremiah is playing with a balance. He fills one bucket with variously sized Lego blocks and the other bucket with variously sized wooden blocks. The scale tilts toward the wooden blocks. Jeremiah takes all of the wooden blocks out and the scale tilts toward the plastic blocks. Jeremiah puts two of the biggest wooden blocks back into the bucket and the scale tilts back toward the wooden blocks. He takes the big blocks out and puts 3 small wooden blocks in the bucket. The balance rocks back and forth and settles evenly. Jeremiah looks up at his teacher who has been watching and grins.

Look back at the Georgia Early Learning Standards at the beginning of the chapter.

- What mathematical standards was Jeremiah addressing in his play?
- What do the decisions he made during play show evidence of?
- What questions might a teacher ask to elicit more information about how Jeremiah thought about the mathematics he has already encountered?

What questions might a teacher ask to allow her to assess and Jeremiah to think about other kinds of mathematics?

more complex. However, as the primary grades have become more and more academic, many teachers have few opportunities for observing mathematics in play in the upper primary grades. This said, watching children engage in mathematics informally can still provide important insight into the children's mathematical capabilities, and may be particularly important for children who experience a great deal of anxiety during formal assessments.

Many of the strategies described for finding time for play in the upper primary grades, such as having time set aside on Friday afternoons, before the bell rings in the morning or during indoor recesses, can also be used to find times for assessing the use of mathematics in informal contexts. Teachers in first and second grade may want to target skills that are particularly hard to assess on paper during these opportunities for observation. For example, Ms. Freeman, a 1st-grade teacher, had been trying to encourage her children to count-on when adding rather than counting up. Many of the children in her class were still counting all of the first set of objects in addition to all of the second set; however, it was hard for her to tell from the written work turned in, which children had mastered the skill and which were still struggling. She decided to make a variety of games available in her classroom—some commercially designed and some that she created herself—that all required rolling two to three dice in order to move. She allowed children to play these games in the morning before announcements and during indoor recesses. Through observing children during game play, she was able to identify which children were counting on when adding up the numbers on the dice and which were not. This knowledge let her make targeted decisions about instruction and also to communicate knowledgeably with parents about the mathematical skills their children needed to practice.

In similar ways, opportunities to play with Lego blocks, wooden blocks, pattern block puzzles, and geometric building kits allow teachers to watch the ways that children solve problems and use mathematical language for authentic purposes. In addition, unlike instructional settings, when teachers may be concerned about keeping all children on task, moving efficiently through the lesson, or on making sure no one is bored, play settings provide teachers with enough time to watch particular children and to make judgments about what they know and can do. Figures 9.2 and 9.3 provide opportunities for you to think about how to assess mathematics in play contexts.

DESIGNING PLAY-BASED ASSESSMENT TASKS

In addition to taking anecdotal records for assessment purposes during play, teachers can also consciously design assessment tasks to be used in play contexts or to draw on toys that are familiar to students during play, such as the task described in Figure 9.4. These tasks can be given as part of formal assessment interviews or can be used individually to assess a particular area of mathematics. Often doing assessments in these ways relieves some of the anxiety that some children feel during assessments and may help children perform more competently under these conditions. In thinking about designing these assessments, the key is to think about the mathematics that you wish to assess and the play resources you have in your classroom to see where you can find connections. To get you started, here are a few ideas developed by teachers.

Prekindergarten

About 4 months into the year, Ms. Umezu decided that she needed to check on her children's individual progress in terms of counting and number. Specifically, she wanted to know if her children could recognize

Figure 9.3. Try It Out 2

Tina built this during her indoor recess in 1st grade and her teacher snapped a picture of it.

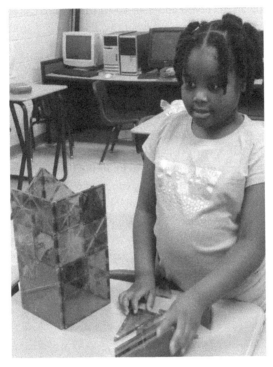

Key Geometry Standards:

- Distinguish between defining attributes (e.g., triangles are closed and three-sided) versus non-defining attributes (e.g., color, orientation, overall size); build and draw shapes to possess defining attributes.
- Compose two-dimensional shapes (squares, triangles, rectangles) and three-dimensional shapes (cubes, right rectangular prisms, right circular cones, and right circular cylinders) to create a composite shape, and compose new shapes from the composite shape.

Questions:

What do you think this child knows or is experimenting with in relation to these standards?

What questions might you ask to elicit the child's thinking about the key standards?

Figure 9.4. Play-Based Assessment in Action

Ms. Chang, a kindergarten teacher, wanted to get a sense of her children's abilities to compose and decompose shapes. Using a Lego board, she used blocks to outline a rectangle on the board and then asked children to use any blocks they chose to fill in the rectangle. Here are what two children did on the assessment.

Ellie

When Ellie sat down, she immediately picked up a piece as long as the outer edge of the rectangle, tried to put it inside and found that it didn't fit. She said out loud, "It's too big. I need a square." She hunted in the blocks for a medium sized square. When she placed it inside the rectangle, it filled half the open space. She then spotted two small narrow rectangle blocks and said, "Hey! I can use these." She put them in one on top of the other to fill in the remaining space. Ms. Chang asked, "Can you tell me about the blocks you used to fill in the rectangle." Ellie said, "I used a square and two little rectangles." Ms. Chang asked, "What shape did the two little rectangles make?" Ellie grinned. "Another square." From this interaction, Ms. Chang could tell that Ellie was able to accurately use vocabulary to name shapes and that she was able to compose and decompose a simple shape fluently, with little reliance on trial and error. She was ready for more complex tasks.

Bryan

When Bryan sat down to do the same task, he began by picking up a long rectangle. He tried to fit it in one way and then the other. He then picked up a small rectangle and put it right in the middle of the open space, which made it difficult for him to find blocks to fill in around it. To try to do it, he picked up one block after another, attempting to push it into the space with little effort to estimate which blocks would best fit. He looked up at Ms. Chang and said, "It doesn't work." She asked him to look in the blocks and see if he could find any skinny ones that might fit. Bryan dug around in the blocks for a moment before shaking his head. Ms. Chang selected some of the skinny blocks and helped him to fit them into the empty space. When she finished, she asked him to tell her about the blocks he had used. He said, "I used some red and a blue one." Through this interaction, Ms. Chang could see that Bryan needed more experiences with both geometry vocabulary and with composing and decomposing shapes. She knew that working with wooden blocks, which are larger and easier to manipulate than the Lego blocks, would be productive for him and planned to make sure that he had opportunities to play with those blocks in the upcoming weeks.

written numerals, correctly count sets of objects 1–10 (K.CC.B.5), and correctly identify sets of more or less (K.CC.C.6). She also wanted to check to see if any of her children had developed the cardinality principle—in other words, to see if they realized the last number of a counting sequence named the whole set. As a context for the assessment she decided to use a toy farm that the children frequently played with during center time. She stocked the barn with toy animals, including cows, horses, pigs, and chickens. She then made a field on a green piece of paper and used white blocks to make fences to create pens for each of the animals. When she brought out the barn at center time, many children were curious about it and wanted to play. Ms. Umezu assured them that everyone was going to get to help her plan a farm, but they would have to do it one at a time. Then, while her paraprofessional supervised the children's play, Ms. Umezu invited the children over one at a time to work with her. She told them that all of the animals had been jumbled up in the barn during a wind storm and that some of the animals had even blown over from the farm next door. She told the children that the farmer had left a letter asking for their help. She then:

- Asked the students to count out three cows, four horses, seven pigs and ten chickens. (She told the children the extra animals belonged to the neighbor.) After the student counted each set, Ms. Umezu asked the child "How many are there in all?" This allowed her to assess the cardinality principle.
- Asked the students to assign the animals to a pen and label that pen with a card that had the correct number on it. Students chose from cards numbered 0–10.
- Asked the children to identify which pen had the most animals and which had the least. She then gave them a bowl of extra cows and horses and asked the children to take out enough so the neighbor would have the same number of cows and horses as the farmer.

Altogether, this activity took about 5–10 minutes with each child. Ms. Umezu had a checklist on her clipboard so she was able to quickly mark off what each child could do, and while a similar assessment could have been done at a table with counting cubes, by using a toy and a story, Ms. Umezu made the activity more attractive and enjoyable to the children in the room.

Kindergarten

Mr. Buxton, a teacher in a school with many children who were learning to speak English as a second language, was concerned that using written assessments with his students might not capture what they knew about mathematics, even if he read the questions aloud to them so he was starting to experiment with performance assessments where he could meet with each child and find ways to support students in communicating about what they knew. Early in the year, he decided to develop an assessment to see where his students were in learning to correctly identify shapes regardless of orientation (K.G.A.2), to use positional language (such as above, below and beside) (K.G.A.1), and to compose simple shapes to form larger shapes (K.G.B.6). He decided to use pattern block puzzles as the focus of his assessment, beginning by allowing children to play with the materials in any way they wanted. He then presented a series of outlines for the children to fill in with blocks, beginning with outlines that had the color of each block shown and ending with a drawing that had only the edge of the shape. After students completed each puzzle, Mr. Buxton asked students to tell him about the pictures they made. He listened to see which shape words and positioning words the children used. If they did not use appropriate vocabulary, he probed them, both by using the words in their home language or by using cards with drawings of shapes on them and asking the children to identify similar shapes in their puzzles. In doing this assessment, not only was Mr. Buxton able to create a more related environment for students, but he was able to see when students could recognize similar shapes regardless of orientation or could compose complex shapes, even if they had not yet developed the vocabulary necessary to describe what they were doing.

1st Grade

Mrs. Dunham wanted to assess her 1st-graders' abilities to compose and decompose numbers into 10s and 1s (1.NBT.B.2). She decided to set up a "store" in the back of her classroom with buckets of items leftover from various craft projects, including puffballs, stickers, jewels, sequins, pipecleaners, and so on. She asked students to come back one at a time and choose three buckets. She then asked students to take a handful of materials and then to count them using groups of ten to organize them. Finally, she asked students to look at the materials they had organized, write down the correct number to represent each pile and organize those numbers from least to greatest. Mrs. Dunham stored each child's materials in a plastic bag so that when the whole class had completed the assessment, each child could create an art project with the items they had chosen. Mrs. Dunham did the first couple of children herself to make sure that the assessment was productive, but she then trained one of her parent volunteers to conduct the assessment, taking notes on any mistakes the child made counting and noting whether the numbers the child wrote were correct. In doing this, Mrs. Dunham both gathered the information she needed about her children's mathematical thinking, but also involved a parent in a meaningful aspect of the classroom. Most children in the class enjoyed the assessment because of the one-on-one attention and because they found the materials attractive, liked handling them, and looked forward to the artwork.

2nd Grade

Miss Freeman, a 2nd-grade teacher, was finishing a unit on linear measurement and rather than give her students a formal test, she decided to do a play-based performance assessment. The children had been planting a garden in science, so Miss Freeman invited her students to make a family of worms out of play dough. She instructed them to make five worms of all different lengths. As the children rolled the play dough into worms, they talked to each other about their worm families, assigning them names, jobs, roles in the family, and personalities. Miss Freeman then handed out a paper for the children to trace their worms organized from largest to smallest. She then passed out another paper that asked students to estimate the length of each of the worm drawings in centimeters and inches, to measure the length of each drawing in centimeters and inches and to figure out how much longer the longest worm was than each of the two smallest worms. These were all skills Miss Freeman needed to assess based on her district curriculum, and while she could have assessed them by simply giving students a series of lines to measure, by locating the assessment in the creation of the worm family, she not only made the task more pleasurable to her students, but also more engaging for many of them.

Currently, even in the earliest grades both parents and children are feeling a lot of anxiety about school assessments. Young children hear older siblings talking about school and may already feel afraid when asked to take tests. Incorporating play into assessments can help both teachers and children relax, which in turn can make it easier to see what it is that children know and still need to learn.

CHAPTER 10

Conclusion

Hopefully, you are now convinced of the empirical benefits of including play in your classroom. However, you might still feel nervous about the reactions that you will get from parents or from administrators. There are of course a variety of approaches that you could take in response to your anxiety, including closing the door and hoping for the best. Certainly, this is a tried and true approach and one you may find necessary at some point. However, it is probably worth your time to invite others to share your vision of humane and effective early childhood pedagogy.

First, you might consider the many synonyms for play: exploration, creative problem solving, drama, choice time, construction, arts-based learning, modeling, building and design, experimentation, physical education, and so on. If you think a schedule that includes blocks of time for two or three of the previously listed activities might elicit a better reaction from adults than a 60-minute block of play time, then by all means change the name. However, as you change the name, remember to make sure the activity retains its playful nature by allowing students to make choices and to linger over their projects.

Second, you might consider sharing reading materials with administrators, other teachers, and even with parents. Sometimes, even if others don't read the texts you provide, they are reassured to learn that you are drawing on a knowledge base.

Figures 10.1 and 10.2 list popular books and relatively accessible journal articles that you may find helpful to share with others. This technique of sharing written texts is particularly helpful when paired with grounded experiences of what children are doing in the classroom.

I have found two ways of sharing with parents and other educators to be particularly helpful. First, encouraging the parents to do some playing with their children with classroom materials during curriculum nights and open houses can change minds. Consider leaving out tubs of blocks,

Figure 10.1. Recommended Books on Play

Play: How It Shapes the Brain, Opens the Imagination, and Invigorates the Soul by Stuart Brown

The Power of Play: Learning What Comes Naturally by David Elkind

Einstein Never Used Flashcards: How Our Children Really Learn—and Why They Need to Play More and Memorize Less by Kathy Hirsh-Pasek and Roberta Michnick Golinkoff

Figure 10.2. Easy-to-Read Journal Articles on Play

Anderson, C. (2010). Blocks: A versatile learning tool for yesterday, today, and tomorrow. *Young Children, 65*(2), 54–56.

Olga, J., & Waite-Stupiansky, S. (2009). Recess—It's indispensable. *Young Children, 64*(5), 66–69.

Parks, A. N., & Chang, D. B. (2014). Helping young children see math in play. *Teaching Children Mathematics, 20*(5), 310–317.

Seo, K. (2003). What children's play tells us about teaching mathematics. *Young Children, 58*(1), 28–34.

puppets, play dough, puzzles, and games for parents and children to play with. Then call parents back together to discuss the learning opportunities available in various kinds of play. You can also go on to connect this play to particular standards in both mathematics and literacy.

Another option is (with parent permission) to take video of children playing inside and outside and to show clips to groups of parents (or teachers) as examples of what children can learn in play. I have found that people become very excited and engaged when looking at these clips. For example, I showed a group of parents video clips of their children counting as they hopped down a line on the playground. I pointed out how the children were matching their counts to each hop and connected this to the need to develop one-to-one correspondence. Parents responded that they had never thought about mathematical learning as something that could happen outdoors and were excited to look for opportunities to connect their children's play to mathematics. Incidentally, I have also found that it can be particularly powerful to juxtapose pictures of children at play with pictures of children sitting in their seats doing worksheets (see, for example, Photos 10.1 and 10.2). Few can argue with the startling differences apparent in children's eyes and bodies.

Photo 10.1. Camden Sits Through a Whole-Class Lesson

Photo 10.2. Camden Engaged in Building 3-D Figures

You can also help your students become advocates for play in the classroom. By taking time to debrief play sessions, you can help children develop language to talk about what they did, make connections between their play and the formal curricula, and talk about their day with their parents in ways that emphasize the rich learning opportunities your classroom offers (rather than simply saying "we just played" when asked about the school day).

Finally, you may also need to reassure parents (and administrators) that your children will still have many traditional schooling experiences. Point out the times of day when you do guided literacy lessons, directed science experiments, and pencil-and-paper mathematics problems. Reassure them that not only is there time for learning in both play and formal contexts, but that the learning in both settings is actually more powerful because of the children's diverse experiences.

*   *   *

There is a great deal of evidence supporting the incorporation of play into the classroom, and that evidence can be particularly useful in getting support from administrators and parents. However, research on what works alone cannot guide our actions in the classroom. For example, we could imagine a research study that demonstrated that administering electric shocks to children led to higher test scores. And yet, even in the face of this "evidence," no one would advocate such a practice. We are responsible for asking not just whether a pedagogy works, but also whether it is ethical to use with children.

There are a couple of ways to frame this question in relation to play. The most common ethical argument is probably that using play with young children is developmentally appropriate. For example, in their handbook, the National Association for the Education of Young Children states that "play needs to be a significant part of the young child's day—and part of a developmentally appropriate classroom" (Copple & Bredekamp, 2009, p. 328). To back up this statement, the handbook draws on research such as that described in this book, which demonstrates the physical, social, and cognitive benefits of play for young children. Examples are also provided of instruction that is not developmentally appropriate, such as allotting little or no time for play, drawing heavily on workbooks for instruction, or talking or reading for long periods. From this perspective, play is to be preserved for young children because they are in particular need of it and because other kinds of instructional strategies are not well-suited to small children.

This argument is fine as far as it goes, but many of the practices critiqued in the handbook—having children sit for long periods of time, asking only fact-oriented questions, not taking into account children's ideas, not providing enough time for independent exploration—are harmful to children regardless of age. These practices, which children throughout elementary school find stressful, do not become appropriate because a certain number of birthdays have passed.

I believe teachers need an ethical stance that encourages us to pay attention to the children in our rooms and the impact of our pedagogies on them (not just on their test scores). Mikhail Bakhtin, a Russian philosopher, put forward a theory of ethical behavior designed to draw people's attention to the particular context of each moment they experience with others. In doing this, he was contrasting his view of moral standards with that of German philosopher Immanuel Kant. Kant argued that we should make decisions based on categorical imperatives, working off laws that could be applied universally without regard to particular contexts. From this perspective, we could set guidelines for different grade levels about the amount of minutes of indoor and outdoor play required for children that age and the amounts of seatwork that should be allowed.

In contrast, Bakhtin (1990) said that ethical action cannot be taken without responsiveness to the people in the moment with you. He called this responsiveness "answerability." He wrote:

> I myself—as the one who is actually thinking and who is answerable for his act of thinking—I am not present in the theoretically valid judgment. The theoretically valid judgment, in all of its constituent moments, is impervious to my individually answerable self-activity. (p. 4)

This means that as a teacher I cannot simply turn to guidelines—even developmentally appropriate ones—to decide what it is okay to do in my classroom. If my children are miserable, it is not enough to say that they have had the appropriate amount of play and so must return to seatwork. "I, myself—as the one who is actually thinking" must decide what it is ethical to do based on what I see happening with the children in front of me. This stance calls on us as teachers to see with fresh eyes the children in our classrooms. If they routinely cry, if they get into arguments, if they become impatient or angry, then we must ask ourselves if the conditions of the classroom are in some way responsible. We cannot justify practices that we identify as harmful because they are required in the standards, by the district, or in order for children to be successful in later grade levels. In fact, Bakhtin refers to these outside requirements as *alibis*, and argues that we cannot use them to justify behavior we know to be unethical.

From this perspective, we, as the adults in the classroom with the children, need to take responsibility for our decisions to deny or to allow children opportunities to play. Practically, as we look around our classroom, we can ask the following questions:

- When do the children seem joyful?
- When do they laugh?
- When are they most engaged?
- When do students cry?
- When do they get angry?
- When do I feel happiest and most relaxed?

Attending to these questions pushes us toward the creation of a humane as well as educative classroom environment, and almost certainly toward a classroom that includes time for play. Literacy scholar Deborah Hicks, in discussing Bakhtin's ethics, wrote that the commitment required by answerability was "more similar to faithfulness, even love, than to adherence to a set of norms" (1996, p. 107). As the adults who are responsible for small children for large parts of their lives, we need to bring that faithfulness to our work with them, just as much as our concern for standards or testing outcomes.

Opportunities for Mathematical Learning During Play

Math Concepts	Possible CCSSM	Activities
Number Recognition	K.CC.A.1. Count to 100 by ones and by tens. K.CC.A.2. Count forward beginning from a given number within the known sequence. 1.NBT.A.1. Read and write numerals and represent a number of objects with a written numeral.	Counting board games Magnetic refrigerator numbers Number puzzles
Counting and One-to-One Correspondence	K.CC.B.4.A. When counting objects, say the number names in the standard order, pairing each object with one and only one number name and each number name with one and only one object. 1.NBT.A.1. Count to 120, starting at any number less than 120. 2.NBT.A.2. Count within 1,000. 2.NBT.A.3. Read and write numbers to 1,000.	Board games Counting while drawing Counting while playing with cards Drawing different types of fruit Making unifix sticks Counting toys Playing with play-dough cut-outs
Measurement	K.MD.A.2. Directly compare two objects with a measurable attribute in common to see which object has "more of"/"less of" the attribute. 1.MD.A.2. Express the length of an object as a whole number of length units, by laying multiple copies of a shorter object end to end. 2.MD.A.1. Measure the length of an object by selecting and using appropriate tools. 2.MD.A.3. Estimate lengths using units of inches, feet, centimeters and meters.	Building with unifix cubes and comparing sizes Active games (e.g., bowling, ring toss) Links and chains Fitting bins into limited sized areas

Math Concepts	Possible CCSSM	Activities
Shapes: Recognition and Creation	K.G.A.1. Describe objects in the environment using names of shapes, and describe the relative positions of these objects using terms such as above, below, beside, in front of, behind, and next to. K.G.A.2. Correctly name shapes regardless of their orientations and overall size. 1.GA.1. Distinguish between defining attributes versus non-defining attributes; build and draw shapes to possess defining attributes. 2.G.A.1. Recognize and draw shapes having specified attributes.	Drawing Reading books about shapes Shape puzzles Play-dough cut-outs
Shapes: Composition and Decomposition	1.G.A.1. Compose 2-dimensional shapes or 3-dimensional shapes to create a composite shape, and compose new shapes from the composite shape.	Duplo tower structures Roads made out of blocks Making structures out of blocks
Symmetry	1.G.A.3. Partition circles and rectangles into two and four equal shares, describe shares using the words halves, fourths, quarters.	Block structures Road made out of blocks Drawing Folding blankets and doll clothes
Patterns	M.P.7. Look for and make use of structure.	Creating shape necklaces Links and chains Drawing
Spatial Relations and Relationships	K.G.B.5. Model shapes in the world by building shapes from components. 2.G.A.3. Recognize that equal shares of identical wholes need not have the same shape.	Blanket folding Block Constructions Filling in spaces with blocks Pattern blocks Puzzles

Words to Listen for to Identify Informal Mathematics

Counting Numbers	In front of	Gone
Ordinal Numbers	Behind	Shape words
More	Turn it	Bigger
Less	Over here	Smaller
Equal	Above	Too many
Same	Below	Try again
Take away	Put together	Doesn't fit
Forward	All	Winning/beating
Backward	None	

Observation Form

Center:		Time:
Mathematical Activity to Look For		

Counts objects in set to ___	Explores weight, length, height	Uses names of shapes
Rote counts to ___	Compares objects with measurement	Uses words to describe shape attributes
Names amount in all	Uses tools to measure	Composes and decomposes shapes
Uses same, more, less		
Quickly identifies amount in set	Uses directional language (e.g., above, below, in front, etc.)	

Children			
Name:	Name:	Name:	Name:

References

Bakhtin, M. M. (1990). *Art and answerability: Early philosophical essays*. M. Holquist & V. Liapunov (Eds.), & V. Liapunov (Trans.). Austin, TX: University of Texas Press.

Borko, H., Mayfield, V., Marion, S., Flexer, R., & Cumbo, K. (1997). Teachers' developing ideas and practices about mathematics performance assessment: Successes, stumbling blocks, and implications for professional development. *Teaching and Teacher Education, 13*(3), 259–278.

Burghardt, G. M. (2011). Defining and recognizing play. In A. Pelligrini (Ed.), *The Oxford handbook of the development of play* (pp. 9–18). New York, NY: Oxford University Press.

Caldera, Y. M., Culp, A. M., O'Brien, M., Truglio, R. T., Alvarez, M., & Huston, A. C. (1999). Children's play preferences, construction play with blocks, and visual-spatial skills: Are they related? *International Journal of Behavioral Development, 23*, 855–872.

Casey, B., Andrews, N., Schindler, H., Kersh, J. E., Samper, A., & Copley, J. (2008). The development of spatial skills through interventions involving block building activities. *Cognition and Instruction, 26*(3), 269–309.

Casey, B., Erkut, S., Cedar, I., & Young, J. M. (2008). Use of a storytelling context to improve girls' and boys' geometry skills in kindergarten. *Journal of Applied Developmental Psychology, 29*(1), 29–48.

Casey, B., Kersh, J. E., & Young, J. M. (2004). Storytelling sagas: An effective medium for teaching early childhood mathematics. *Early Childhood Research Quarterly, 19*, 167–172.

Clements, D. H. (2003). *Learning and teaching measurement (2003 Yearbook)*. Reston, VA: National Council of Teachers of Mathematics.

Clements, D. H., Wilson, D. C., & Sarama, J. (2004). Young children's composition of geometric figures: A learning trajectory. *Mathematical Thinking and Learning, 6*(2), 163–184.

Copple, C., & Bredekamp, S. (Ed.). (2009). *Developmentally appropriate practice in early childhood programs: Serving children birth through age 8*. Washington, DC: National Association for the Education of Young Children.

Elkind, D. (2007). *The power of play: Learning what comes naturally*. Philadelphia, PA: Da Capo Lifelong Books.

Enyedy, N., & Mukhopadhyay, S. (2007). They don't show nothing I didn't know: Emergent tensions between culturally relevant pedagogy and mathematics pedagogy. *The Journal of the Learning Sciences, 16*(2), 139–174.

Esmonde, I. (2009). Ideas and identities: Supporting equity in cooperative mathematics learning. *Review of Educational Research, 79*(2), 1008–1043.

Ginsburg, H. (2006). Mathematical play and playful mathematics: A guide for early education. In D. Singer, R. Golinkoff, & K. Hirsh-Pasek (Eds.), *Play = Learning* (pp. 145–165). New York, NY: Oxford University Press.

Ginsburg, H. P., Greenes, C., & Balfanz, R. (2003). *Big math for little kids.* Parsippany, NJ: Dale Seymour Publications.

Ginsburg, H. P., Lee, J. S., & Boyd, J. S. (2008). Mathematics education for young children: What is it and how to promote it. *Social Policy Report of the Society for Research in Child Development, 22,* 3–22.

Graham, T. A., Nash, C., & Paul, K. (1997). Young children's exposure to mathematics: The child care context. *Early Childhood Education Journal, 25*(1), 31–38.

Graue, M. E. (2006). The answer is readiness—Now what is the question? *Early Education and Development, 17*(1), 43–56.

Gregory, K. M., Kim, A. S., & Whiren, A. (2003). The effect of verbal scaffolding on the complexity of preschool children's block constructions. In D. E. Lytle (Ed.), *Play and educational theory and practice* (pp. 117–133). Westport, CT: Praeger.

Guanella, F. M. (1934). Block building activities of young children. *Archives of Psychology, 174,* 5–92.

Gullo, D. F., & Hughes, K. (2011). Reclaiming kindergarten: Part I. Questions about theory and practice. *Early Childhood Education Journal, 38*(5), 323–328.

Hicks, D. (1996). Learning as a prosaic act. *Mind, Culture & Activity, 3*(2), 102–118.

Hirsh-Pasek, K., Kochanoff, A., Newcombe, N. S., & de Villiers (2005). Using scientific knowledge to inform preschool assessment: Making the case for "empirical validity." *Social Policy Report, 19*(1), 3–19.

Kamii, C., Miyakawa, Y., & Kato, Y. (2004). The development of logico-mathematical knowledge in a block-building activity at ages 1–4. *Journal of Research in Childhood Education, 19*(1), 44–57.

Kersh, J., Casey, B. M., & Young, J. M. (2008). Research on spatial skills and block building in girls and boys. In O. N. Saracho & B. Spodek (Eds.), *Contemporary perspectives on mathematics in early childhood education* (pp. 233–251). Charlotte, NC: Information Age Publishing.

Kyle, D. W., McIntyre, E., Miller, K. B., & Moore, G. H. (2002). *Reaching out: A K–8 resource for connecting families and schools.* Thousand Oaks, CA: Corwin Press.

Lakoff, G., & Núñez, R. E. (2000). *Where mathematics comes from: How the embodied mind brings mathematics into being.* New York, NY: Basic Books.

Levine, S. C., Ratliff, K. R., Huttenlocher, J., & Cannon, J. (2012). Early puzzle play: A predictor of preschoolers' spatial transformation skill. *Developmental Psychology, 48*(2), 530.

Lifter, K., & Bloom, L. (1998). Intentionality and the role of play in the transition to language. In A. M. Wetherby, S. F. Warren, & J. Reichle (Eds.), *Transitions in prelinguistic communication* (pp. 161–195). Baltimore, MD: Paul H. Brookes Publishing Company.

Lillard, A. S. (1993). Pretend play skills and the child's theory of mind. *Child Development, 64*(2), 348–371. doi: 10.2307/1131255.

Miller, E., & Almon, J. (2009). *Crisis in kindergarten: Why children need play in school.* College Park, MD: Alliance for Childhood.

National Association of for the Education of Young Children & National Council of Teachers of Mathematics. (2002). Early childhood mathematics: Promoting good beginnings. *Early Childhood Today, 17*(4), 15.

National Governors Association Center for Best Practices. (2010). Common Core State Standards Mathematics. Available at www.corestandards.org.

National Research Council. (2009). *Mathematics learning in early childhood: Paths toward excellence and equity.* Washington, DC: National Academy Press.

Pepler, D. J., & Ross, H. S. (1981). The effects of play on convergent and divergent problem solving. *Child Development, 52,* 1202–1210.

Piaget, J. (1962). *Play, dreams, and imitation in childhood.* London, England: Routledge.

Preston, R., & Thompson, T. (2004). Integrating measurement across the curriculum. *Mathematics Teaching in the Middle School, 9*(8), 436–441.

Purcell, K., Heaps, A., Buchanan, J., & Friedrich, L. (2013). How teachers are using technology at home and in their classrooms. Pew Research Center's Internet & American Life Project. Available at pewinternet.org/Reports/2013/teachers-and-technology

Ramani, G. B., & Siegler, R. S. (2008). Promoting broad and stable improvements in low income children's numerical knowledge through playing number board games. *Child Development, 79*(2), 375–394.

Ramani, G. B., & Siegler, R. S. (2011). Reducing the gap in numerical knowledge between low- and middle-income preschoolers. *Journal of Applied Developmental Psychology, 32,* 146–159.

Sarama, J., & Clements, D. H. (2004). Building blocks for early childhood mathematics. *Early Childhood Research Quarterly, 19*(1), 181–189.

Seo, K. (2003). What children's play tells us about teaching mathematics. *Young Children, 58*(1), 28–34.

Seo, K. H., & Ginsburg, H. P. (2004). What is developmentally appropriate in early childhood mathematics education? Lessons from new research. In D. H. Clements, J. Sarama, & A. DiBiase (Eds.), *Engaging young children in mathematics: Standards for early childhood mathematics education* (pp. 91–104). Mahwah, NJ: Lawrence Erlbaum Associates.

Siegler, R. S. (2009). Improving the numerical understanding of children from low-income families. *Child Development Perspectives, 3*(2), 118–124.

Siegler, R. S., & Ramani, G. B. (2008). Playing linear numerical board games promotes low income children's numerical development. *Developmental Science, 11*(5), 655–661.

Siegler, R. S., & Ramani, G. B. (2009). Playing linear number board games—but not circular ones—improves low-income preschoolers' numerical understanding. *Journal of Educational Psychology, 101*(3), 545.

Smith, S. S. (2006). *Early childhood mathematics*. Boston, MA: Pearson.

Steffe, L., & Cobb, P. (1998). *Construction of arithmetic meanings and strategies*. New York, NY: Springer-Verlag.

Stephan, M., & Clements, D. H. (2003). Linear and area and time measurement in prekindergarten to grade 2. In D. H. Clements (Ed.), *Learning and teaching measurement (2003 Yearbook)* (pp. 3–16). Reston, VA: National Council of Teachers of Mathematics.

Thompson, T. D., & Preston, R. V. (2004). Measurement in the middle grades: Insights from NAEP and TIMSS. *Mathematics Teaching in the Middle School, 9*(9), 514–519.

Tudge, J. R., & Doucet, F. (2004). Early mathematical experiences: Observing young Black and White children's everyday activities. *Early Childhood Research Quarterly, 19*(1), 21–39.

Van de Walle, J. A., Karp, K. S., Bay-Williams, J. M., & Wray, J. (2007). *Elementary and middle school mathematics: Teaching developmentally*. Boston, MA: Pearson.

Vygotsky, L. S. (1978). *Mind in society: The development of higher psychological processes*. Cambridge, MA: Harvard University Press.

Vygotsky, L. S. (1962). *Thought and language*. Cambridge, MA: MIT Press.

Wager, A. A. (2014). Practices that support mathematics learning in a play-based classroom. In L. D. English & J. T. Mulligan (Eds.), *Reconceptualising early mathematics learning* (pp. 163–182). Dordrecht, Germany: Springer.

Wager, A., & Parks, A. N. (2014). Learning mathematics through play. In S. Edwards & M. Blaise (Eds.), *Handbook of play and learning in early childhood* (pp. 216–227). Los Angeles, CA: Sage.

Wang, Z., & Hung, L. M. (2010). Kindergarten children's number sense development through board games. *The International Journal of Learning, 17*(8), 19–31.

White, J. C., & Bull, R. (2008). Number games, magnitude representation, and basic number skills in preschoolers. *Developmental Psychology, 44*(2), 588.

Wiggins, G. P., & McTighe, J. (2005). *Understanding by Design*. Alexandria, VA: Association for Supervision and Curriculum Development.

Wolfgang, C., Stannard, L., & Jones, I. (2003). Advanced constructional play with Legos among preschoolers as a predictor of later school achievement in mathematics. *Early Child Development and Care, 173*(5), 467–475.

Wolfgang, C. H., Stannard, L. L., & Jones, I. (2001). Block play performance among preschoolers as a predictor of later school achievement in mathematics. *Journal of Research in Childhood Education, 15*(2), 173–180.

Index

About the Author

Amy Noelle Parks is a former elementary school teacher and the mother of two daughters. She is currently an associate professor of Mathematics Education at Michigan State University. Much of her thinking for this book was informed by 5 years of research and professional development at a rural school in Georgia that serves primarily African American children. Broadly, her research focuses on the mathematical learning of young children in both formal and informal contexts.